(LISP 1.5 PRIMER
    (BY
        (CLARK WEISSMAN)))

DICKENSON SERIES IN COMPUTER AND INFORMATION SCIENCE

Fred M. Tonge, Editor

(LISP 1.5 PRIMER
(BY
(CLARK WEISSMAN)))

Programming Systems Staff Head
Research and Technology Division
System Development Corporation

DICKENSON PUBLISHING COMPANY, INC., BELMONT, CALIFORNIA

Library of Congress catalog card number: 67-20611

Printed in the United States of America

PREFACE

The original LISP programming system was implemented at M.I.T.[1] based
upon a paper by John McCarthy, "Recursive Functions of Symbolic Expressions
and Their Computation by Machine," which was published in Communications of
the ACM, April 1960. Since then, numerous other LISP systems have been implemented on a variety of computers.[2,3,4,5,6] All these systems are based
upon the formal LISP language; however, they do possess differences in
implementation brought about by machine differences and technological advances
in efficient machine utilization. Earlier systems used interpreters for
evaluating LISP expressions; more recent systems compile machine code to perform
the desired symbolic manipulations. Other technological innovations, such as
time-sharing operating systems, have also influenced the outward, user-view of
LISP systems. To transcend these and other differences between LISP systems,
various pedagogical devices are used in this manual. Hopefully, these devices
will approximate features available with specific LISP implementations. They
include: a compiler-based LISP 1.5 system, an EVALQUOTE supervisor, a full
complement of character handling primitives, MACRO capability, and a canonical
form for input and output of numbers, atoms, and symbolic expressions.

The primer starts simply with a formal definition of a symbolic expression, its
syntax and graphical representation. Two alternative machine-readable notations
are defined for representing symbolic expressions. Once the student becomes
familiar with recognizing symbolic expressions, he learns how to take them apart
into smaller elements or put them together into larger expressions using the
elementary LISP functions CAR, CDR, and CONS. The early chapters of this book
are essential to the understanding of LISP. They expose the reader to the
LISP formalism and give him an opportunity to acquire the necessary skills for
processing symbolic data. Learning these skills is analogous to learning the
rules of arithmetic.

Lambda expressions are introduced immediately after the fundamentals of symbolic
expressions. Lambda expressions are the basic functional syntax of LISP. LISP
functions are analogous to procedures used in algebraic languages, and derive

directly from the mathematics of recursive function theory. The concepts of evaluation and quoting are established and used to explain the nature of EVALQUOTE, the "universal" LISP function and system supervisor that can compute the value of any computable function applied to its arguments.

Conditional expressions, predicates, and arithmetic functions add control and computational power to the language and complete the set of basic expressions that may be composed in LISP. At this point recursion is introduced.

Recursion is a technique for defining a computation on a given datum. The process usually produces a partial solution and reduces the datum to a simpler form. The same process is then reapplied to this simpler form of the datum. Again a partial solution and a simpler form are obtained. The process continues until some terminal datum obtains, whereupon all partial solutions are combined in some fashion to produce the final solution. To compute recursively the factorial of N, for example, we have

$$N! = N * (N-1)!$$

where N is the partial solution and (N-1) is the simpler form upon which we repeat the factorial computation. This process recurs until the terminal condition N = 0 is reached, whereupon the partial results are combined to form the final answer; e.g.,

$$N * (N-1) * (N-2) * \ldots 3 * 2 * 1$$

Recursion is as natural to symbolic data manipulation as iteration is to numerical data processing. LISP is designed to make recursion easy to use, and recursive functions are a significant part of the domain of LISP expressions. Since numerical data is also allowed in LISP, iterative functions can be defined using the PROG feature, in which statements are evaluated in ALGOL-like serial fashion.

Beyond Chapter 15, the primer is devoted to advanced techniques for extending the domain of symbolic expressions using functional arguments, macros, property lists, and list structures. Also, this portion of the primer describes input-output, and delves more deeply into the nature of variables, values and their

association. The last chapter provides a review of foregoing chapters by
describing a complete LISP program that differentiates an algebraic polynomial.

LISP is not an easy language to learn because of the functional syntax and
insidious parenthetical format; this is particularly true for those experienced
with more conventional programming languages. However, LISP is consistent in
its syntax no matter how complex the expression. Careful attention to this
fact may make learning easier. The carefully graduated sets of exercises can
help in this regard. They have been selected for use with or without a computer.
They may be used on-line if a time-sharing system is at hand. Otherwise, the
solutions given in Appendix A can be used for comparison. These solutions have
been computer-checked for accuracy and correctness.

Santa Monica, California   Clark Weissman
December, 1966

ACKNOWLEDGMENTS

I wish to acknowledge the considerable support I received from the System Development Corporation in preparing an earlier version of this text for the AN/FSQ-32 computer time-sharing system.

Kudos to Dr. Daniel G. Bobrow of Bolt, Beranek and Newman and to Michael Levitt of Systems Concepts for their perseverance in reviewing the text and for their suggestions regarding technical content and presentation. Thanks are extended to Robert Wills of SDC for his editorial help and for linearizing my oft-times "recursive" English grammar. Thanks also to Patricia Gicie for carefully counting parentheses as she typed and retyped the many final manuscripts.

To Dr. Stanley Kameny, Robert Saunders, Donna Firth, Jeff Barnett, Dr. Marvin Minsky, all my students, and others in the LISP community, my sincere appreciation for their enthusiastic reception of the earlier version of the primer; for their suggestions based upon trial experience; for contributing exercises, and for checking technical consistency.

Above all, I wish to thank my wife, Marcia, for her encouragement, self-imposed exile and the patient care she bestowed on me during the preparation of this manuscript.

Clark Weissman

TABLE OF CONTENTS

Page

CHAPTER 1.
INTRODUCTION

1.1   PURPOSE OF THIS DOCUMENT

This manual has two principal goals: (1) to introduce the programming language
LISP and present a systematic exposition of symbolic computation, and (2) to
serve as a self-tutor for those wishing to acquire a practical facility with
the LISP 1.5 programming language.

LISP is an unusual language in that it is both a formal mathematical language,
and (with extensions) a convenient programming language. As a formal mathematical language, it is founded upon a particular part of mathematical logic known
as recursive function theory. As a programming language, LISP is concerned
primarily with the computer processing of symbolic data rather than numeric data.

From childhood we are exposed to numbers and to ways of processing numerical
data, such as basic arithmetic and solutions to algebraic equations. This
exposure is based upon a well-established and rigorously formalized science of
dealing with numbers. We are also exposed to symbolic data--such as names,
labels, and words--and to ways of processing such data when we sort, alphabetize,
file, or give and take directions. Yet the processing of symbolic data is not
a well-established science. In learning an algebraic programming language, such
as FORTRAN or ALGOL, we call upon our experience with numbers to help us understand the structure and meaning (syntax and semantics) of the language.

In learning a symbolic programming language such as LISP, however, we cannot call
upon our experience, because the formalism of symbolic data processing is not
part of this experience. Thus, we have the added task of learning a basic set
of formal skills for representing and manipulating symbolic data before we can
study the syntax and semantics of the LISP 1.5 programming language.

LISP is designed to allow symbolic expressions of arbitrary complexity to be
evaluated by a computer. To achieve a thorough understanding of the meaning,
structure, construction, and evaluation of symbolic expressions, is to learn

how to program in LISP. This primer seeks to develop such understanding gradually by building new material upon older material, and by expanding the scope of definition of prior concepts. The primer provides a practical foundation for understanding the programming language; supplemental readings can then augment the material presented here.

1.2   DOCUMENT CONVENTIONS

In the narrative portions of this manual, certain elements of LISP can easily be confused with normal English. To help clarify word and phrase usage from sample LISP code, a number of conventions are followed herein.

When reference is made specifically to LISP elements, LISP syntax, or LISP semantics, the first occurrence of a significant term or definition is signified by the use of italics. An example, defined in the next chapter, is the term *S-expression*.

Most LISP program examples, parts of programs, and function and variable names are typed in capital letters, analogous to the form of input accepted by LISP systems from keypunched card decks or on-line keyboards. Certain other program examples contain a mix of capital letters and italicized letters. In such cases, the italics are used to denote "meta-linguistic" variables that are not part of the LISP language, but are used in the accompanying text to describe legal LISP forms. An example, discussed in Chapter 6, is the form of a lambda expression:

(LAMBDA *varlist body*)

where the meta-variables *varlist* and *body* aid in describing the syntax of lambda expressions. Also the ellipsis (...) is not part of the LISP language, but merely a device used for designating a sequence of indefinite length. Lower-case elite letters are also used in many cases as "pedagogic" variables or examples of legal classes. These are used to aid in describing the semantics of a given expression. For example, in Chapter 11, the conditional expression

$$(COND \ (p_1 \ e_1) \ (p_2 \ e_2) \ \cdots \ (p_n \ e_n))$$

uses p_i and e_i as such pedagogic variables.

When a programming example is given, it is usually separated from the body of the text and placed on a separate line without normal English punctuation, exactly as it might be entered into the computer. At other times, explicit references to code and function or variable names are capitalized and imbedded in the text; all normal English punctuation may then be used.

Finally, underscoring is occasionally used to emphasize or draw the reader's attention to a particular point.

1.3   LISP APPLICATIONS

LISP enlarges the problem-domain to which computers may be applied by extending the nature of mathematical objects beyond numbers, to include a great variety of structures and the processes for computing with them. As a general programming language, LISP can be applied to a wide variety of non-numerical, mixed numerical, and symbolic data processing problems.

The problem-domain is typically characterized by problems with "ill-defined" data requirements. These problems have data that change dynamically in size and content as the problem moves nearer solution. Also, the structure of the data is as important as its content. Hierarchical structures are most common; however, linear lists of numbers, arbitrary character strings, and paired objects are frequently required. Problems with these data characteristics encompass iterative and recursive computational algorithms for solution.

More specifically, LISP has been applied to problems in machine checking of mathematical proofs, inductive inference on sequences, computations in particle physics, meta-compilers, pattern matching string transformations, programming language syntax translation, integral and differential calculus, electrical circuit theory, game playing, simulation, question/answering systems, linguistics, information retrieval, graphics and display programming, and on-line, interactive text editing.

The new expansion of man's view of the nature of mathematical objects, made possible by LISP, is exciting. There appears to be no limit to the diversity of problems to which LISP will be applied. It seems to be a truly general language, with commensurate computing power.

CHAPTER 2.
SYMBOLIC EXPRESSIONS

All programs and data in the LISP programming language are in the form of
symbolic expressions usually referred to as *S-expressions*. S-expressions are
of indefinite length and have a branching binary tree structure, so that significant sub-expressions can be readily isolated. The bulk of available memory
in a computer is used for storing S-expressions in list-structure form. This
type of memory organization frees the programmer from the necessity of allocating
storage for different sections of his program or data. It also makes LISP
programs and data homogeneous (i.e., programs can be treated as data and vice
versa by other programs), a unique feature of the language.

2.1   ATOMIC SYMBOLS

The most elementary type of S-expression is called an *atomic symbol* or an *atom*.
Atoms may be numeric or non-numeric. (We will discuss numeric atoms later.)
Non-numeric atoms are called *literal atoms*.

Definition:

> A literal atom is a string of capital letters and
> decimal digits of indefinite length, the first
> character of which is a letter.[†]

Examples:

> A
> APPLE
> PART2
> EXTRALONGSTRINGOFLETTERS
> A1B66X4ZZ

These symbols are called atomic because they are taken as a whole and are not
viewed as individual characters. Thus A, B, and AB are three distinct and
unrelated atomic symbols.

[†] Some recent LISP implementations have liberalized this definition. They accept
as literal atoms any character string that cannot be interpreted as a number.

2.2   DOT NOTATION

All non-atomic S-expressions are written in what is called *dot notation*. They are built of atomic symbols and the punctuation marks:

> (left parenthesis
>
>)   right parenthesis
>
> .   period or dot

These larger S-expressions (non-atomic S-expressions) are always parenthesized and always have two parts—a left part and a right part. A dot is used to delimit the two halves. For example, the S-expression

> (A . B)

has atomic symbol A as its left part, and atomic symbol B as its right part. Thus, a non-atomic S-expression is always a *dotted pair*.

Definition:

> An S-expression is either:
> 1. An atom, e.g., A1
> 2. A dotted pair of atoms, e.g., (A . B)
> 3. A dotted pair of S-expressions, e.g., ((A . B) . C)

The general form of a dotted pair is: a left parenthesis, an S-expression, one or more spaces, a dot, one or more spaces, an S-expression, and a right parenthesis.

Notice that in this definition an S-expression is defined in terms of itself. We speak of this as a "recursive" definition.

Examples:

> ATOM
> (A . B)
> (A . ATOM)
> (ATOM1 . (BETA . C))
> ((U . V) . X)
> ((U . V) . (X . (Y . Z)))

2.3   GRAPHICAL REPRESENTATION OF DOTTED PAIRS

All non-atomic S-expressions are internally represented as a binary tree structure, i.e., a tree structure with but two branches at each node. It is often helpful to the student to "see" the graphical representation of this tree structure.

We assume the following graphical symbols and their associated meanings:

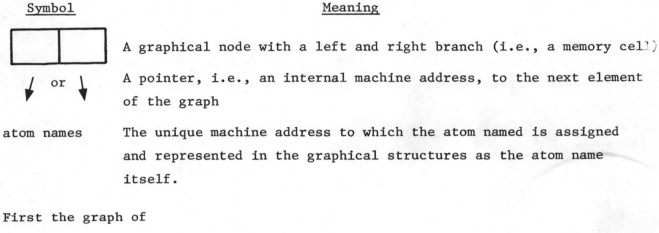

Symbol   Meaning

A graphical node with a left and right branch (i.e., a memory cell)

A pointer, i.e., an internal machine address, to the next element of the graph

atom names   The unique machine address to which the atom named is assigned and represented in the graphical structures as the atom name itself.

First the graph of

(A . B)

is given by

where the left part of the dotted pair, atom A, is named in the left branch of the node, and the right part of the dotted pair, atom B, is named in the right branch of the node.

The graph of

((A . B) . C)

is slightly more complicated, namely

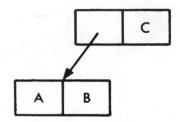

In this case, the left branch of the higher node points to the lower node, while the right branch of the higher node contains the name of atom C. The lower node is exactly the graph of

(A . B)

shown above because it is the same S-expression. In this example, however, it is a sub-expression of the S-expression

((A . B) . C)

We see here graphically the meaning of sub-expression: it is an S-expression at a lower level and appears in dot notation as a more deeply parenthesized S-expression.

<u>Examples</u>:

(A . (B . C))

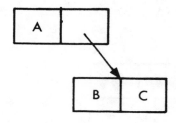

((A . B) . (C . D))

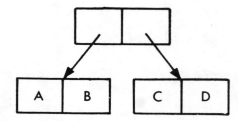

(A . (B . (C . D)))

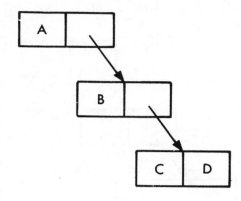

(((A . B) . C) . D)

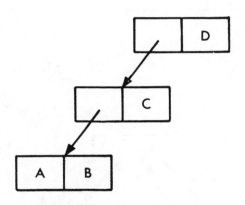

((((A . B) . C) . D) . (DD . (CC . (BB . AA))))

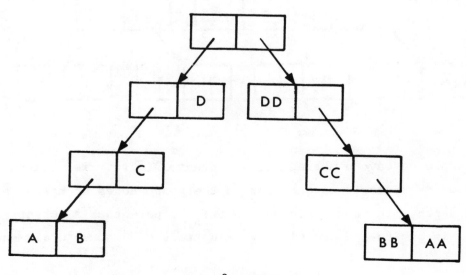

$$((((A \cdot B) \cdot (A \cdot B)) \cdot (A \cdot B)) \cdot (A \cdot B))$$

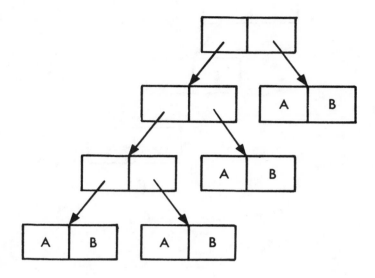

$$((((A \cdot B) \cdot (C \cdot D)) \cdot (E \cdot F)) \cdot (G \cdot ((H \cdot I) \cdot (J \cdot K))))$$
$$1234 \quad 4 \quad 4 \quad 43 \quad 3 \quad 32 \quad 2 \quad 34 \quad 4 \quad 4 \quad 4321$$

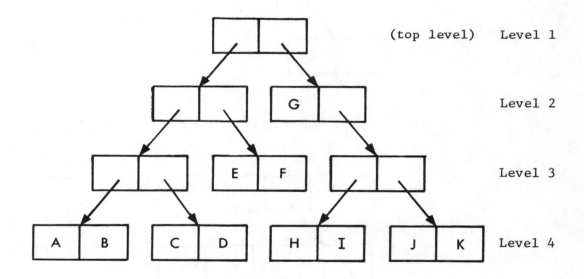

In this example we have numbered the parentheses (a tutorial aid that is not a legal part of S-expressions) and labeled the graph nodes according to their sub-expression depth. The correspondence between a parenthesis subscript and a graph level is one-to-one and clearly illustrates the structural meaning of the

S-expression. With more complicated S-expressions we have a deeper and larger
graph. Thus, we can see that S-expressions can be of unlimited size and complexity, constrained only by the physical memory capacity of the computer.

2.4   <u>EXERCISES</u>

Which of the following are atomic symbols?

    1.   ATOM
    2.   A B
    3.   A1B2C3
    4.   NIL
    5.   (X)
    6.   LISP
    7.   Q32
    8.   ONE
    9.   (MY . NAME)
    10. 2TIMES

Identify the dotted pairs.

    11.   A . B
    12.   X . Y . Z
    13.   (YOU . AND . ME)
    14.   (X . Y)
    15.   (NIL . NIL)

Graph these dotted pairs.

    16.   (ONE . (TWO . THREE))
    17.   (((THREE . NIL) . TWO) . ONE)
    18.   ((A . B) . (B . (C . D)))

What S-expressions are these structures?

19.

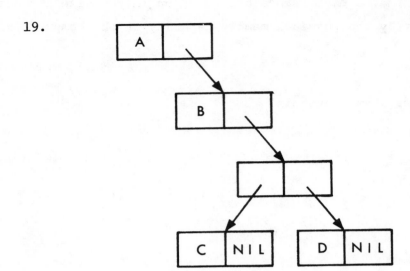

20.

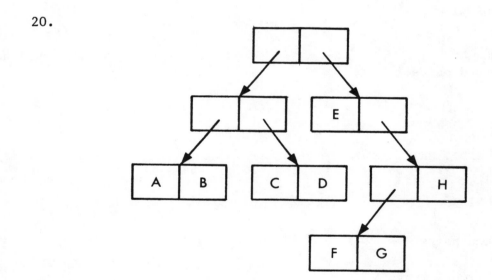

CHAPTER 3.
SYMBOLIC EXPRESSIONS IN LIST NOTATION

Dot notation is necessary and sufficient to represent <u>all</u> list structures in LISP, and, in fact, is the fundamental concept upon which the programming language is built. However, it leaves much to be desired as a convenient programming notation for S-expressions, particularly because of its excess of parentheses and dots. *List notation* was invented to improve this situation and simplify the reading and writing of S-expressions.

For example, the *list*

(A B C D)

is an S-expression in list notation for the same S-expression

(A . (B . (C . (D . NIL))))

written in dot notation. (The atom NIL has special significance and will be discussed shortly.)

3.1   LIST ELEMENTS

A list may have sublists, and these sublists may also have sublists. It is usually convenient to speak of *elements* of a list. An element then may be an atom, a list of atoms, or a list of lists. A list of lists is called a *list structure*.

For example, (A B C) is a list with three atomic elements, A, B, and C, whereas (A (B C)) is a list of two elements, the atom A, and the list (B C). The second element, (B C), is a list of two atomic elements, B and C. Finally, the list structure ((A) (B) (C)) is a list of three elements, the lists (A), (B), and (C).

Historically, the separator for elements of lists was the comma; however, one or more blanks or spaces are now generally used. Either is acceptable.

Thus, the two S-expressions

$$(A \ B \ C \ D)$$

and

$$(A,B,C,D)$$

are entirely equivalent in LISP.

The student should be cautioned that though much of the LISP programming language is written in list notation, the basis for this form is always dot notation. In fact, all S-expressions in list notation can be transformed into their dot-notation equivalents, but not all S-expressions in dot notation can be transformed into list notation. This will be evident after we examine the rules and identities required for translating between notations.

3.2   NIL

About the turn of the century, theoretical physics was in a dilemma. Was light emission a wave or a particle phenomenon? Ample evidence existed to support either school of thought. Physics resolved its dilemma by considering light as a wavicle.

LISP also has a dilemma, resolved in a similar fashion. The dilemma derives from the flexibility of lists to represent data sequences of arbitrary length. To properly manipulate lists, it is imperative that some convention exist for recognizing the end of a list.

For example, consider the list (A B). If we remove the first element, we have the remaining list, (B). If we again remove the first element, we have the remaining list, ( ). This is the terminal point of the original list, (A B). It is the *empty list*. The empty list is the LISP convention for the end of a list, and it is defined as the atom NIL.

Like the wavicle of physics, NIL is simultaneously an atom and a list. LISP programmers can use either "spelling", ( ) or NIL, as they are identically represented internally by LISP. We consider NIL, not the last element of a list, but the terminator of a list.

-14-

3.3   TRANSFORMING LIST NOTATION TO DOT NOTATION

All non-atomic S-expressions are defined as dotted pairs. It is therefore possible to transform a list to its equivalent form in dot notation. The following rules and identities define the transformation.

Identity 1:

> A list of one atom is a dotted pair of the atom and NIL, with NIL always the right part of the dotted pair, i.e.,

$$(atom) \equiv (atom \ . \ NIL)$$

or equivalently

$$(atom) \equiv (atom \ . \ (\ ))$$

Examples:

$$(A) \equiv (A \ . \ NIL)$$
$$(EXTRALONGATOM) \equiv (EXTRALONGATOM \ . \ NIL)$$
$$\left.\begin{array}{c}(NIL) \\ ((\ ))\end{array}\right\} \equiv \left\{\begin{array}{c}(NIL \ . \ NIL) \\ ((\ ) \ . \ (\ ))\end{array}\right.$$

When transforming a multi-element list to its equivalent form in dot notation, we begin by composing the dot notation equivalent for only the top-level elements of the list. We then compose the dot notation equivalent for each sublist, and so on until the list is completely transformed to dot notation. All we need then is a rule for transforming a simple list to its dot notation equivalent, repeating that rule for all sublists. We can now state that rule.

Rule 1:

> The first (left-most) list element, when transformed to dot notation, is always the left part of a dotted pair. If the first element is also the last element of the list, by Identity 1, it is dotted with NIL. If the first element is not the last element of the list,

then the right part of the dotted pair is the list
formed by removing the first element. Then apply
Rule 1 to the right part of the dotted pair.

For example, given the list

$$(A\ B\ C)$$

we apply Rule 1 and get

$$(A\ .\ (B\ C))$$

Since

$$(B\ C)$$

is the right part of the dotted pair and is itself a list, we apply Rule 1
again to get

$$(A\ .\ (B\ .\ (C)))$$

Again, the right part is a list (C) so we apply Rule 1 once more. We note,
however, that the list (C) satisfies Identity 1 and is equivalent to

$$(C\ .\ NIL)$$

Hence, the final S-expression is given by

$$(A\ .\ (B\ .\ (C\ .\ NIL)))$$

For another example, the list

$$(A\ (B\ C)\ D)$$

yields these partial expansions for each application of Rule 1.

$$(A\ .\ ((B\ C)\ D))$$
$$(A\ .\ ((B\ C)\ .\ (D)))$$
$$(A\ .\ ((B\ C)\ .\ (D\ .\ NIL)))$$

Now, expanding the sublist (B C) we find

$$(A \: . \: ((B \: . \: (C)) \: . \: (D \: . \: NIL)))$$
$$(A \: . \: ((B \: . \: (C \: . \: NIL)) \: . \: (D \: . \: NIL)))$$

Examples:

(A B C)	$\equiv$	(A . (B . (C . NIL)))
((A B) C)	$\equiv$	((A . (B . NIL)) . (C . NIL))
(A B (C D))	$\equiv$	(A . (B . ((C . (D . NIL)) . NIL)))
((A))	$\equiv$	((A . NIL) . NIL)
((NIL))	$\equiv$	((NIL . NIL) . NIL)
(())	$\equiv$	(NIL . NIL)
(A (B . C))	$\equiv$	(A . ((B . C) . NIL))

From the above examples you can see that Identity 1 can be stated alternatively as: When converting from list to dot notation, the only atom that appears adjacent to a right parenthesis is NIL.

3.4   TRANSFORMING DOT NOTATION TO LIST NOTATION

It is _always_ possible to convert list notation to dot notation, since S-expressions are defined by dot notation. However, we _cannot_ always convert dot notation to list notation. For example, we cannot transform

$$(A \: . \: B)$$

The rule that is in effect follows from Identity 1.

Rule 2:

> Only those dotted pairs in which the only atom
> adjacent to a right parenthesis is NIL can be
> represented in list notation.

For complicated dotted pairs, the following procedure can be followed starting with any dotted pair:

1. If the right part of the dotted pair is an atom and not NIL, conversion to list notation is impossible.

2. If the right part of the dotted pair is non-atomic (i.e., a list or a dotted pair) or NIL—treat NIL here as ()—then

    a. delete the last right parenthesis of the dotted pair
    b. delete the dot
    c. delete the first left parenthesis of the right part; the left part thereby becomes the first element of the list
    d. repeat the procedure on the remaining dotted pairs.

For example, given the dotted pair

(A . (B . NIL))

the most nested dotted pair is

(B . NIL)

Representing NIL by ( ) and applying the procedure above, we find

(A . (B))

Applying the procedure again, we get the list

(A B)

For the case

(A . ((B . C) . (D . NIL)))

repeated application of the procedure yields these expressions:

(A . ((B . C) . (D)))
(A . ((B . C) D))
(A (B . C) D)

We can reduce this list no further, as the second element of the list

(B . C)

is a dotted pair that cannot be represented as a list. We call the expression

$$(A \; (B \; . \; C) \; D)$$

a list, but recognize that it is in mixed notation. Mixed notation is perfectly acceptable to LISP and is quite common in LISP S-expressions.

3.5   GRAPHICAL REPRESENTATION OF LISTS

Lists can be transformed into their equivalent dot notation; graphical representation of dotted pairs is covered in Section 2.3. This section will review that material, but with the introduction of NIL.

Inasmuch as NIL is an atom, we need not introduce any new graphical symbology. However, since we use NIL as a list terminator, a diagonal slash is often used to represent NIL, and is adopted here. Thus the graph for

$$(A \; . \; NIL)$$

is

But

$$(A \; . \; NIL) \equiv (A)$$

so the graph also shows a single element list.

For more complicated lists, we shall show the list, its dotted pair equivalence, and its graph.

List	Dotted Pair
(A B C)	(A . (B . (C . NIL)))

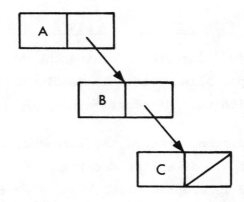

((A) B C)	((A . NIL) . (B . (C . NIL)))

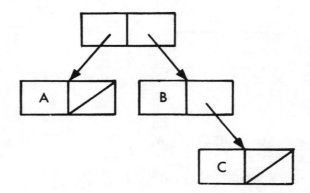

List	Dotted Pair
(A (B) C)	(A . ((B . NIL) . (C . NIL)))

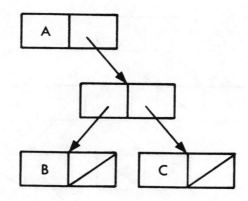

List	Dotted Pair
(A B (C))	(A . (B . ((C . NIL) . NIL)))

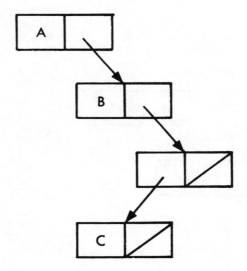

List	Dotted Pair
((A) (B) (C))	((A . NIL) . ((B . NIL) . ((C . NIL) . NIL)))

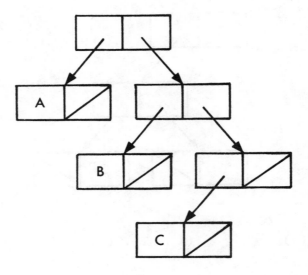

(((A B)))	(((A . (B . NIL)) . NIL) . NIL)

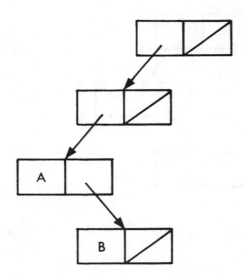

3.6   EXERCISES

Transform these lists to their fully expanded dot notation equivalents.

1. (ATOM)
2. ((LISP))
3. (((MORE YET)))
4. (HOW ABOUT THIS)
5. (DONT (GET (FOOLED)))

Now go the other way--dotted pairs to lists.

6. (X1 . NIL)
7. (NIL . (X1 . NIL))
8. (KNOW . (THY . (SELF . NIL)))
9. ((BEFORE . (AND . (AFTER . NIL))) . NIL)
10. (A . (((B . (C . NIL)) . NIL) . NIL))

To what S-expressions do these graphs correspond?

11.

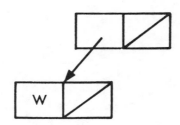

12.

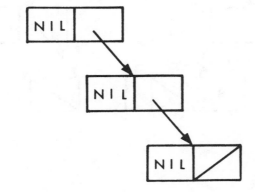

13.

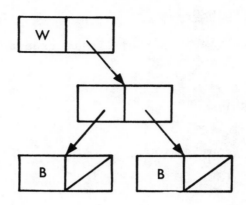

14.

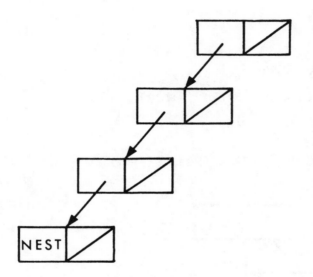

15.

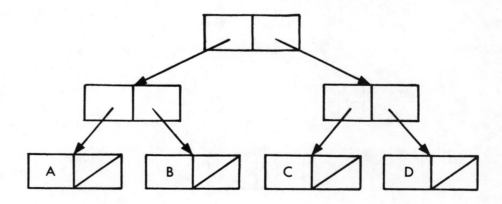

CHAPTER 4.
NUMBERS

In LISP, numbers are atoms and may be used in S-expressions exactly as the previously defined literal atoms are used. Thus,

(1 2 3 A 4 B 5)

or

(ALPHA . 960)

are legal S-expressions.

Since LISP systems are implemented on many different computers with varying hardware features, the conventions for legal numbers differ widely. All implementations accept integer and octal fixed-point numbers. Systems on larger machines also accept floating-point numbers. All octal numbers end with the letter "Q" to distinguish them from integers. Floating-point numbers follow scientific notation, which includes a decimal point and an optional decimal scale factor distinguished by the letter "E". Beyond these simple, general features, you should consult your particular LISP system reference literature for its number conventions.

This chapter stipulates a set of syntax conventions used consistently throughout the primer. Because of the likelihood that these conventions will clash with those of your system, care has been taken, in the balance of the primer, to avoid examples and exercises that depend on this pedagogy.

4.1   INTEGER NUMBERS

Fixed-point numbers are positive or negative integers, with or without a scale factor. The scale factor is denoted by the letter "E", followed by a blank or any positive integer. Negative scaling is illegal and not meaningful for fixed-point numbers. Thus,

796E-17

is unacceptable for LISP.

LISP Number	Meaning
123	+123
+123E0	+123
−321E	−321
−1E3	$-1 \times 10^3 = -1000$
53E0	+53

4.2 OCTAL NUMBERS

Integers may also be represented in octal. Octal numbers are denoted by octal digits, followed by the letter "Q", followed by a blank or any positive <u>decimal</u> integer. The Q <u>must</u> be present. The decimal integer following Q is a scale factor showing the power of eight. Negative scale factors are illegal and not meaningful for octal or decimal numbers.

Thus,

75757Q−4

is unacceptable for LISP.

The largest octal number allowed is a machine−dependent characteristic. A machine having 48 bits per word has been assumed for all LISP arithmetic in this primer. Implementations of LISP on machines with lesser word length will yield numerical results having fewer significant digits than given here.

Examples:

LISP Number	Meaning
123Q	123×8^0
123Q2	123×8^2
777Q3	777×8^3
2Q8	2×8^8
3Q10	3×8^{10}

4.3   FLOATING-POINT NUMBERS

Floating-point numbers must contain a decimal point. Floating-point numbers may
be positive or negative, with an optional scale factor. The scale factor is
always denoted by the letter "E", and may be followed by a blank or any
positive or negative integer.

Examples:

LISP Number	Meaning
3.14159	+3.14159
+1.0E-3	+0.001
-976.003E3	-976003.00
0.273E+2	+27.30
23.E-1	+2.30
17.	+17.00

4.4   DECIMAL POINT OR DOTTED PAIR RESOLUTION

When floating-point numbers are used in S-expressions, the computer can be
confused as to the meaning of the period. Is it treated as a decimal point or
as the dot in a dotted pair? To eliminate confusion and avoid ambiguity, always
surround the dot with blanks when writing a dotted pair, and never surround
the decimal point with blanks when writing a floating-point number.

For instance,

(1.2.3.4)

is an illegal S-expression. Whereas

(1.2 . 3.4)

is perfectly proper.

4.5   <u>EXERCISES</u>

Which of the following are S-expressions?

    1.   (Q . 1Q)

    2.   (5E . (E . NIL))

    3.   (E5 . 5E)

    4.   (1.E . 1Q)

    5. Q3

    6. 4.4

    7.   (A.9)

    8.   (B . 9.9)

    9.   (9.9.9)

  10.   (1.23 77Q3 27 27E5 0.321E-7 ALPHA Q) . 32)

Convert the following to list notation, if possible.

  11.   (99.9 . NIL)

  12.   (NIL . 99.9)

  13.   ((PI) . 3.14159E0 . NIL)

  14.   (5 . (5.5 . (5Q5 . (55.0E-1 . (5E2 . NIL)))))

  15.   ((13.13 . NIL) . ((25Q2 . NIL) . NIL))

CHAPTER 5.
ELEMENTARY FUNCTIONS

LISP is a language for manipulation of S-expressions. Fundamental to this manipulation is the ability to build S-expressions from smaller S-expressions and produce sub-expressions from a given S-expression. These abilities are possible with the elementary LISP functions CONS, CAR, and CDR.

5.1   RAPPORT WITH THE SUPERVISOR

Before we examine the elementary functions, we must understand a basic element of the syntax of the communication language accepted by the LISP system. Chapter 9 covers the subject in greater detail. At this juncture we will only consider the requisite parenthesization.

When we input to the LISP system, we are communicating with a supervisor program that always expects <u>two</u> inputs, both S-expressions. If we call this pair of S-expressions s_1 and s_2 respectively, the first S-expression, s_1, is always treated by the supervisor as:

1. The name of a function, or
2. An S-expression that behaves as a function.

(We will focus on the former case here, and examine the latter case in subsequent chapters.) Since functions have arguments, the second S-expression, s_2, is <u>always a list of the arguments for the function</u> whose name is the S-expression s_1.

Consider the trigonometric function

$$SIN\ 90^{\circ}$$

If SIN were a LISP function, we would write

$$SIN\ (90)$$

where the first S-expression, s_1, is SIN and the second S-expression, s_2, is the list (90)--the list of the single argument required by SIN.

As another example, in LISP the function PLUS performs the operation of addition of its arguments. We can compute the sum of three numbers by giving the following pair of S-expressions to the supervisor:

$$\underbrace{\text{PLUS}}_{s_1} \quad \underbrace{(1\ 2\ 3)}_{s_2}$$

The S-expression s_1 is the name of the function PLUS. The S-expression s_2 is a list with three elements (i.e., 1, 2, 3), each an argument for the function PLUS.

5.2   CONS

CONS refers to "the construct of" and is the function that is used to build S-expressions. It has two arguments that are both S-expressions.

Definition:

> The CONS of two S-expressions is the dotted pair
> of these S-expressions, with the first S-expression
> being the left part, and the second S-expression
> being the right part of the dotted pair.

For example, given the arguments A and B, we can CONS them by giving the supervisor

$$\underbrace{\text{CONS}}_{s_1} \quad \underbrace{(\text{A}\ \text{B})}_{s_2}$$

which means (A . B).

If the arguments were the lists (A) and (B), we would write

$$\underbrace{\text{CONS}}_{s_1} \quad \underbrace{(\ (\text{A})\ (\text{B})\ )}_{s_2}$$

which is equivalent to

$$((\text{A})\ .\ (\text{B})) = ((\text{A})\ \text{B}) \quad ?$$

-30-

<u>Examples</u>:

$$\text{CONS(M N) = (M . N)}$$
$$\text{CONS((A . B) C) = ((A . B) . C)}$$
$$\text{CONS(A (B C D)) = (A . (B C D)) = (A B C D)}$$

5.3   <u>CAR</u>

CAR (pronounced "car") is one LISP function used to extract a sub-expression from an S-expression. Its meaning is "the first of." It has <u>one</u> argument, a <u>non-atomic</u> S-expression (i.e., a dotted pair, or a list).

<u>Definition</u>:

> The CAR of a <u>non-atomic</u> S-expression is the <u>left</u> part of the S-expression when represented in dot notation, or the <u>first element</u> of the S-expression when represented in list notation. <u>The CAR of an atom is undefined.</u>

For example, the CAR of the argument (M . N) would be written

$$\underbrace{\text{CAR}}_{s_1} \underbrace{(\ (\text{M . N})\ )}_{s_2}$$

which is equivalent to M. Note that for this example the list s_2 is ((M . N)), a list of one element--the single argument for the function CAR.

<u>Examples</u>:

$$\text{CAR((A . B)) = A}$$
$$\text{CAR(((A . B) . C)) = (A . B)}$$
$$\text{CAR((A B C D)) = A}$$
$$\text{CAR(((A B C) D E)) = (A B C)}$$
$$\text{CAR(FOO) = undefined for atoms}$$

5.4   CDR

CDR (pronounced "could-er") is another LISP function used to extract a sub-expression from an S-expression. Its meaning is "the rest of". It has <u>one</u> argument, a <u>non-atomic</u> S-expression similar to that accepted by CAR. CAR of a given non-atomic S-expression yields the first element of an S-expression; CDR yields the rest of that S-expression after the CAR is removed.

<u>Definition</u>:

> The CDR of a <u>non-atomic</u> S-expression is the <u>right part</u> of the S-expression when represented in dot notation, or the balance of the S-expression after the first element is removed when represented in list notation. <u>The CDR of an atom is undefined</u>.

For example, the CDR of the argument (M . N) would be written

$$\underbrace{\text{CDR}}_{s_1} \; (\; \underbrace{(M \; . \; N)}_{s_2} \;)$$

which is equivalent to N.

Do not confuse list and dot notation when evaluating the CDR. If the CAR of list

        (A B)

is removed, the remainder is still a <u>list</u>, i.e., (B).

If the CAR of the dotted pair

        (A . B)

is removed, the remainder is the right part, B.

Thus,

$$CAR \ ((A \ . \ B)) = A$$
$$CDR \ ((A \ . \ B)) = B$$
$$CAR \ ((A \ B)) = A$$
$$CDR \ ((A \ B)) = (B)$$

Examples:

$$CDR((A \ . \ Y)) = Y$$
$$CDR((A \ . \ (ATOM))) = (ATOM)$$
$$CDR((A \ B \ C \ D)) = (B \ C \ D)$$
$$CDR(FOO) = \text{undefined for atoms}$$

Note: The CDR of a list with only one element, e.g., (A), is the atomic symbol NIL. For example:

$$CDR((A)) = (\ ) = NIL$$

5.5   GRAPHICAL INTERPRETATION OF CAR AND CDR

In the previous chapters we examined the graphs of LISP S-expressions and noted the binary tree structure of these expressions. Let us now examine the meaning of the elementary functions that operate on these tree structures.

If someone asked for directions to get to your home, you would most naturally couch such directions in terms of city blocks, and house numbers. In LISP, we are faced with a similar problem—to provide the LISP system with directions for "traveling" through the binary tree structure of an S-expression. We couch such directions in terms of CAR and CDR, which designate the appropriate "turn" at each binary "fork in the road".

For example, given the S-expression

$$((A \ B) \ C \ D) = ((A \ . \ (B \ . \ NIL)) \ . \ (C \ . \ (D \ . \ NIL)))$$

its graph is given by

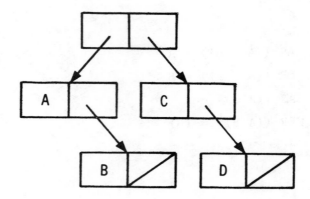

The CAR and CDR of this S-expression yield

$$CAR \ (\ ((A \ B) \ C \ D) \ ) = (A \ B)$$
$$CDR \ (\ ((A \ B) \ C \ D) \ ) = (C \ D)$$

In the graph we note that

$$(A \ B)$$

is the left branch of the top node and

$$(C \ D)$$

is the right branch. The connecting arrows of this graph were called *pointers* in Chapter 2.

We see now that they are pointers to the CAR and CDR. We often say they point to the "CAR chain" or "CDR chain" of the structure. If we take the CAR and CDR repeatedly at each node, we can completely "traverse" the S-expression, and reach any sub-expression or atom of the original S-expression. The following graph is completely labeled according to these CAR and CDR directions, and the "location names" of each pointer.

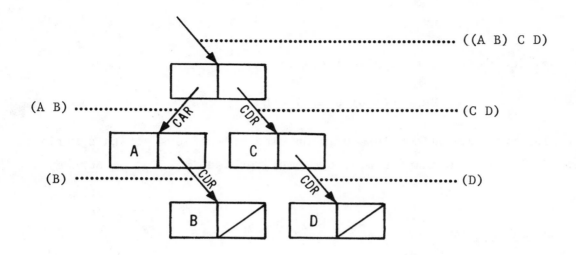

To get from the original S-expression to the atom D, we require the following
directions:

1. CDR (((A B) C D)) = (C D)
2. CDR of the output of (1), i.e.,

    CDR ((C D)) = (D)

3. CAR of the output of (2), i.e.,

    CAR ((D)) = D

A standard convention, more fully covered in subsequent chapters, is to define
and name a class of new functions that perform these successive CAR, CDR operations. For each function in the class, the naming convention is to concatenate
the names of all the CAR, CDR operations to be applied into one uniquely spelled
abbreviation. The abbreviation rule uses the common letters "C" and "R" as
the start and end characters of the name. Various combinations of the letters
"A" (for CAR), and "D" (for CDR), constitute the balance of the spelling. The
order of the letters in combination follows directly from left to right, the
order of application of the CAR, CDR operations, from last to first. Thus,
for the above example

                        CAR CDR CDR

yields the name

CADDR

and the new function may be applied; e.g.,

CADDR (((A B) C D)) = D

Much of LISP programming consists of composing "directions" of this variety. Problems 21-31 of this chapter give us some exercise in "finding our way home".

5.6   EXERCISES

Evaluate the following functions:

    1.   CAR((LEFT . RIGHT))
    2.   CDR((LEFT . RIGHT))
    3.   CONS(LEFT RIGHT)
    4.   CAR((A B C D))
    5.   CAR(((A) B C D))
    6.   CAR((A (B C D)))
    7.   CAR(((A . B) C D E))
    8.   CDR((THIS SENTENCE IS A LIST))
    9.   CDR((HOW (ABOUT THIS)))
   10.   CDR(((DOT . PAIR1) (DOT . PAIR2)))
   11.   CONS(CAR CDR)
   12.   CDR((EMPTY))
   13.   CDR((CAR CDR))
   14.   CAR(((CAR) CDR))
   15.   CONS(A ( ))
   16.   CONS(75Q 100)
   17.   CAR((1 . (2.0 . (30.0E-1 . 77Q))))
   18.   CDR((1 . (2.0 . (30.0E-1 . 77Q))))
   19.   CONS((A . B) NIL)
   20.   CAR((((((ALPHA))))))

Note: Problems 1, 2, and 3 above demonstrate the relationship among CONS, CAR, and CDR. Can you state this relationship?

List from <u>right to left</u> the sequence of CAR-CDR LISP functions which, when each is applied to the value of the prior function, will find the "A" in each of the following S-expressions. For example:

CAR CDR

is the answer for the argument (C A T) by the following reasoning:

CDR ((C A T)) = (A T)

then

CAR ((A T)) = A

Q.E.D.

This sequence may be abbreviated as follows:

CAR CDR = CADR
CAR CAR CDR = CAADR
CDR CDR CAR = CDDAR

21. ((C A T))
22. ((A))
23. (M A R T)
24. (B . A)
25. (S M A R T)
26. (1 2Q 3E3 A)
27. ((A . B) (C . D))
28. ((B . A) (C . D))
29. (((C)) ((A)))
30. ((X . Y) (A . B))
31. ((X . Y) (B A))

CHAPTER 6.
LAMBDA NOTATION

In LISP 1.5, as in other programming languages, we wish to write programs that are parameterized and that compute answers when values are assigned to the parameters of the program. However, in LISP 1.5, we do not use the syntax and program structure of algebraic languages. LISP programs are conceived and written with mathematical rigor based upon the formalism of recursive function theory. As such, procedures are functions; parameters are constants and variables that can be passed between functions as arguments; and computation is a process of evaluating S-expressions consisting of functions applied to their arguments.

6.1 FORMS AND FUNCTIONS

Given the algebraic expression

$$y^x$$

evaluate the expression for the values 3 and 4.

For this problem statement, we immediately see a notational problem. Is x=3 and y=4, or vice versa? The value of the expression changes with our assumption. To resolve this ambiguity we need a notation that explicitly states the correspondence between variables and their values. LISP uses such a notation, the *lambda notation*, of Alonzo Church.[7]

In Church's lambda notation the expression

$$y^x$$

is called a *form*. In LISP 1.5 this form would be written as

    (EXPT Y X)

where the format is given in Polish prefix notation. (LISP programmers prefer calling this format "function notation", where the function always precedes its arguments.)

Furthermore, in Church's lambda notation

$$f = \lambda(x,y) \ (y^x)$$

is a *function* named f, since it provides the two necessary ingredients for a function:

1. A form to be evaluated, and
2. A correspondence between the variables of the form and the arguments of the function.

If we now ask the value of the function f for

$$f(3,4)$$

the previous ambiguity is resolved, as Church's lambda notation explicitly gives the number and order of the arguments of f and defines the correspondence of 3 with x, and 4 with y such that

$$f(3,4) = 4^3 = 64$$

In LISP, f(3,4) could be written as

$$\underbrace{(\text{LAMBDA } \underbrace{(X\ Y)}_{\substack{\text{list} \\ \text{of} \\ \text{variables}}} \ \underbrace{(\text{EXPT } Y\ X))}_{\text{form}}}_{s_1} \ \underbrace{(3\ 4)}_{s_2}$$

where s_1 is called a *lambda expression*. A lambda expression is a *functional expression*, i.e., an S-expression that acts like a function. We shall explore lambda expressions more fully below.

6.2 LAMBDA EXPRESSIONS

Definition:

> A *lambda expression* is an S-expression. This S-expression is a <u>list</u> of three elements in the following order:

1. The word LAMBDA

2. A list of literal atoms that may be used as variables
    in the form. These atoms are called *lambda variables*

3. The form

The general syntax accepted by LISP is:

$$(LAMBDA \quad varlist \quad body)$$

where *varlist* is the list of the literal atoms used as variables (*varlist* may
be empty, i.e., NIL), and *body* is any LISP form. For example:

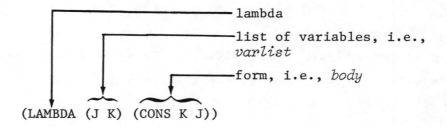

A lambda expression is a functional expression and may be used wherever
functions are acceptable in forms. <u>A lambda expression acts like a function</u>
since it specifies the correspondence between the variables in the form and
the arguments of the function. Therefore, it can be applied to arguments just
as the elementary functions CONS, CAR, and CDR were used earlier.

<u>Examples</u>:

A number of simple lambda expressions are described below.
They are simple because they have elementary forms; however,
they show pertinent properties of lambda expressions that
hold true for all lambda expressions.

1. (LAMBDA ( ) 1)   This is a lambda expression with no
lambda variables, i.e., *varlist* is
NIL. The form is the numerical
constant 1.

2. (LAMBDA (X) 1)   This lambda expression has X as the
                                    only lambda variable. Again, the form
                                    is the numerical constant 1. This
                                    example shows that it is not necessary
                                    for the variable to appear in the form.

3. (LAMBDA (X ANYNAME Y2) 1)   This lambda expression is analogous to
                                    example 2, but with three lambda varia-
                                    bles. It further shows that lambda
                                    variables may be arbitrary literal atoms.

4. (LAMBDA (X) X)   This lambda expression has X as the only
                                    lambda variable. Also, the form is the
                                    lambda variable itself.

6.3   LAMBDA CONVERSION

With Church's lambda notation, both the form and the correspondence between
variables of the function and their values are made explicit by the syntax
of lambda expressions. A lambda expression is the definition of a function.

When a function is called to compute a value from a given set of arguments,
its definition is used to properly associate variables with arguments. After
pairing of variables with arguments (a process called *binding* of variables)
the form is evaluated with the current variable bindings. This process of
binding variables and then evaluating the form inside the lambda expression is
called *lambda conversion*.

The importance of lambda conversion cannot be over-stressed. It is the method
by which all lambda expressions are evaluated, and all called functions receive
their arguments. The conditions and mechanics for lambda conversion are given
below.

Conditions:

1. A lambda expression definition must exist, as either an explicit
    lambda expression, or as a "built-in" function, e.g., a previously
    compiled function.

2. Only literal atoms may be used as lambda variables in the definition. (In subsequent chapters, we shall see that the literal atoms T and NIL may not be used as lambda variables.)

3. The number of arguments in the function call must agree with the number of lambda variables. If there are no lambda variables, i.e., *varlist* is NIL, we have a function of no arguments.

Mechanics:

1. Lambda variables are paired with their corresponding arguments. The order is important since the first lambda variable is paired to the first argument; the second lambda variable is paired to the second argument; etc. This pairing binds the variable to the argument.

2. The form is evaluated.

For example, consider the evaluation of the following top-level (i.e., supervisor level) function call:

$$\underbrace{(\text{LAMBDA (J K) (CONS J K))}}_{s_1} \quad \underbrace{(A\ B)}_{s_2}$$

This function call yields the same value, (A . B), as the top-level call

$$\underbrace{\text{CONS}}_{s_1} \quad \underbrace{(A\ B)}_{s_2}$$

However, since CONS is a built-in function, the former example more clearly demonstrates the mechanics of lambda conversion.

When using a lambda expression at the top level, the lambda expression is the first S-expression, s_1, of the pair presented to the supervisor. Again, the second S-expression, s_2, of the pair is the list of arguments for s_1; in this case, the list of arguments for the lambda expression. It is important to understand that the arguments in the list, s_2, are paired with the lambda variables of the lambda expression, s_1. The arguments in the list, s_2, are matched in number and position with the variables in the list of variables following the LAMBDA. Thus, by lambda conversion, the variable J is paired with the argument A, and the variable K with the argument B. Then the form

$$(CONS\ J\ K)$$

within the lambda expression is evaluated. The bindings of variables J and K are retrieved to yield A and B, respectively; it is these values to which CONS is applied to yield the dotted pair, (A . B).

Examples:

$$(LAMBDA\ (X)\ X)\ (123Q) = 123Q$$
$$(LAMBDA\ (ABLE)\ (CAR\ ABLE))\ (\ (THIS\ IS\ A\ LIST)\ ) = THIS$$
$$(LAMBDA\ (\ )\ 77)\ NIL = 77$$
$$(LAMBDA\ (ONE\ TWO)\ (CONS\ TWO\ ONE))\ (A\ B) = (B\ .\ A)$$
$$(LAMBDA\ (K)\ (CADAR\ K))\ (\ ((1\ 2\ 3)\ 4\ 5)\ ) = 2$$

6.4   PARENTHESES

The lambda expression

$$(LAMBDA\ (A\ B)\ (CONS\ A\ B))$$

uses six parentheses. They are very important. They designate scope or extent of expressions, i.e., where they begin and where they end. Parentheses have to be very precisely positioned. In order to understand them, we shall first number them in associated pairs:

```
(LAMBDA (A B) (CONS A B))
1       2 2         21
```

The first left parenthesis (No. 1) tells the LISP system that this is the start of an expression. The final right parenthesis (No. 1) tells the system that this is the end of the expression.

The first left parenthesis marks the beginning of the scope of the LAMBDA, i.e., the extent of the expression to which LAMBDA applies. The second No. 1 parenthesis marks the end of the scope of LAMBDA.

The second left parenthesis No. 2 marks the beginning of the scope of CONS, with the last parenthesis No. 2 ending that scope.

All parentheses in the S-expressions of LISP always occur in pairs of left and right parentheses; generally, each pair marks the scope of an expression, or bounds a list. The parentheses in LISP are never optional as they are sometimes in mathematics; they are required parts of expressions.

Note that in the example above, the sub-expressions

(A B)

and

(CONS A B)

are both bounded by parenthesis-pairs labeled No. 2. If we consider the parenthesis numbers as "depth" counters or "levels", we see that these two sub-expressions are at the same depth, namely level two. Since the only occurrences of parentheses No. 1 completely bracket the lambda expressions, we say that the lambda expression is at level one.

Parenthesis counting is a good "crutch" in that it immediately identifies sub-expressions at the same level within a larger S-expression--a very useful debugging and formatting tool. In fact, LISP printouts are usually formatted or "pretty printed" by the system, which indents sub-expressions according to their level. This indenting scheme is also a useful aid for entering input to LISP.

6.5   DUMMY VARIABLES

Before we leave lambda expressions, note the following expressions:

(LAMBDA (A B) (CONS A B)) (Q R) = (Q . R)   [1]

(LAMBDA (J K) (CONS J K)) (Q R) = (Q . R)   [2]

The two expressions evaluate to the same value. More importantly, the systematic substitution of J and K for A and B, respectively, in expression [1] translates that expression to expression [2], without changing the form or its meaning. This

is a significant part of Church's lambda notation. Thus, almost any literal
atom will suffice as a variable in a lambda expression. So we speak of them
as *dummy variables*.

6.6   EXERCISES

For the following function calls, give the variable bindings resulting from
lambda conversion.

1.   (LAMBDA (X) X) (ATOM)

2.   (LAMBDA (Y) Y) ((LIST))

3.   (LAMBDA (J) (CAR J)) ((THREE ELEMENT LIST))

4.   (LAMBDA (K) (CDR K)) ((THREE ELEMENT LIST))

5.   (LAMBDA (U V) (CONS U V)) (VERY GOOD)

6.   (LAMBDA (Y X) (CONS Y X)) (ONE (THEN . ANOTHER))

7.   (LAMBDA (A) (CAADR A)) ((A (B . 77Q2)))

8.   (LAMBDA (VARIABLE) (CDAR VARIABLE)) (((A B)))

9.   (LAMBDA (J) 3.14159) (NIL)

10.   (LAMBDA ( ) 3.14159) ( )

11.   (LAMBDA (U V) U) (ALPHA BETA)

12.   (LAMBDA (U V) U) (BETA ALPHA)

13.   (LAMBDA (U V) V) (ALPHA BETA)

14.   (LAMBDA (V U) V) (ALPHA BETA)

15.   (LAMBDA (FIRST SECOND) (CAR FIRST)) ((FIRST) SECOND)

CHAPTER 7.
ELEMENTARY FORMS

Computation in LISP is done by simply evaluating forms. <u>All</u> forms have value, whether they be simple numerical constants, variables, or deeply nested S-expressions. The value of a form is the result of evaluating it; the form is evaluated only once--no more, no less.

If we view lambda conversion in LISP from a more conventional programming stand-point, forms look like programs or "pieces" of a program; an ALGOL "block" is an example. Arguments look like data for these blocks. Since LISP processes symbolic data represented as S-expressions, data in LISP are S-expressions. Note a very significant point: forms are themselves S-expressions, and thus, can be data. We speak of this fact as the "homogeneity of programs and data" in LISP--a unique and powerful feature of LISP. By proper separation of con-text, programs can generate other programs as data. The LISP compiler itself is a LISP program that does just that. In Chapter 19, we shall examine MACRO, a function that does nothing else but transform forms into other forms.

These considerations are brought up to provide motivation for discussing LISP forms at this time. To help the beginner comprehend LISP forms, this chapter and the next two chapters treat (in order) elementary forms, composed forms, and special forms.

7.1   VARIABLES

All variables are elementary forms. In the preceding chapter, we encountered lambda variables. In subsequent chapters we shall consider other variables. Regardless of their origin, variables are elementary forms.

The process of evaluating an elementary form which is just a variable is one of simply retrieving the binding of the variable and returning that binding as the value of the form. With lambda variables, the binding retrieved is the binding established by lambda conversion. In the lambda expression

(LAMBDA (X) X)

the lambda variable X is the form. If we call this function

$$(LAMBDA\ (X)\ X)\ (A)$$

with the argument A, by lambda conversion X is bound to A and the form is evaluated by simply retrieving that binding.

7.2   CONSTANTS

All constants are elementary forms. Since LISP allows numerical and symbolic data, there can be numerical and symbolic constants. All numbers are constants in LISP. In addition, most LISP implementations have T and NIL as symbolic constants for ease of programming conditional expressions (as we shall see in Chapter 11). Apart from these cases, any S-expression may be "quoted" to make it a symbolic constant. Quoting is performed by the special form QUOTE described in Chapter 9.

The process of evaluating an elementary form which is just a constant is one of simply returning that constant as the value of the form. Constants, as in all programming languages, provide a way of representing data within programs.

7.3   SIMPLE FORMS

Simple forms in LISP consist of a left parenthesis, a function name, parameters, and a right parenthesis. Syntactically, this looks like

$$(fname\ parameters)$$

where *fname* is the name of a built-in function, and *parameters* may be one or more variables or constants. In fact, *parameters* may be empty (i.e., there may be no variables or constants) if *fname* is a function of no arguments.

To illustrate, the simple form X^2 is written in LISP as

$$(EXPT\ X\ 2)$$

where EXPT is the *fname*, and variable X and constant 2 are *parameters*. Other examples include

```
(CONS T NIL)
(CAR X)
(CDR ABLE)
(NOARGFUNCTION)
```

The process of evaluating a simple form is as follows:

1. All *parameters* are evaluated: constants evaluate to themselves;
    variables evaluate to their bindings.

2. The atom following the left parenthesis (i.e., *fname*) is assumed
    to be the name of a built-in function. That function is called
    with the values of the *parameters* as arguments.

3. The value of a simple form is the value of the function applied
    to the arguments.

For the simple form

```
(CONS T NIL)
```

the *parameters* are the symbolic constants T and NIL, which evaluate to themselves. CONS is called with these values to yield the value (T . NIL).

For the lambda expression

$$\underbrace{\text{(LAMBDA (ABLE BAKER) (CONS ABLE BAKER))}}_{s_1} \quad \underbrace{\text{(A B)}}_{s_2}$$

lambda variables ABLE and BAKER are bound to A and B, respectively, by lambda
conversion. Then the simple form

```
(CONS ABLE BAKER)
```

is evaluated. The *parameters* of the simple form are variables that evaluate
to their bindings, A and B. CONS is then applied to these arguments to yield
the value (A . B).

7.4   <u>EXERCISES</u>

Try evaluating these lambda expressions:

    1.   (LAMBDA (X) X) (ATOM)

    2.   (LAMBDA (Y) Y) ((LIST))

    3.   (LAMBDA (J) (CAR J)) ((THREE ELEMENT LIST))

    4.   (LAMBDA (K) (CDR K)) ((THREE ELEMENT LIST))

    5.   (LAMBDA (U V) (CONS U V)) (VERY GOOD)

    6.   (LAMBDA (Y X) (CONS Y X)) (ONE (THEN . ANOTHER))

    7.   (LAMBDA (A) (CAADR A)) ((A (B . 77Q2)))

    8.   (LAMBDA (VARIABLE) (CDAR VARIABLE)) (((A B)))

    9.   (LAMBDA (J) 3.14159) (NIL)

   10.   (LAMBDA ( ) 3.14159) ( )

Note:

            Problems 1 and 2 are "identity" functions in that
            they always evaluate to their arguments. Problems
            9 and 10 are "constant" functions which always
            evaluate to the constant specified, in this case
            3.14159, regardless of the value of the argument.
            However, these arguments are required by lambda
            conversion. Also, the supervisor expects a pair
            of S-expressions at the top level. Further, note
            that the list of variables in problem 10 is empty.
            In LISP, a function with an empty variable list is
            a function of no arguments. For proper LISP syntax,
            we must always include the list of variables, even
            when empty. In such cases, NIL is as acceptable
            as ( ).

Evaluate:

   11.   (LAMBDA (U V) U) (ALPHA BETA)

   12.   (LAMBDA (U V) U) (BETA ALPHA)

   13.   (LAMBDA (U V) V) (ALPHA BETA)

   14.   (LAMBDA (V U) V) (ALPHA BETA)

   15.   (LAMBDA (FIRST SECOND) (CAR FIRST)) ((FIRST) SECOND)

CHAPTER 8.
COMPOSITION OF FORMS

To apply LISP to more complex problems, we must be able to create more powerful programs, i.e., more complex forms. This chapter takes a major step in that direction. It generalizes the concept of a simple form by introducing composition of forms.

8.1 COMPOSED FORMS

Recall that a simple form has the syntax

$$(\textit{fname parameters})$$

If we let *args* stand for zero or more elementary or composed forms, we can write down the syntax for a composed form as

$$(\textit{fname args})$$

It follows from this syntax that, if *fname* is CAR and *args* is the elementary form (CDR J), then

$$(CAR \ (CDR \ J))$$

is a composed form. It also follows from the recursive nature of the syntax that, if *fname* is CONS and *args* is the composed form (CAR (CDR J)), then

$$(CONS \ (CAR \ (CDR \ J)) \ (CAR \ (CDR \ J)))$$

is a composed form. By similar reasoning, any depth of composition is possible.

Definition:

> Form composition is the concatenation of forms
> in such a fashion that an argument for a function
> at level n is the value resulting from the
> evaluation of a form at level n + 1.

8.2   EVALUATING COMPOSED FORMS

The process of evaluating a composed form is recursive. If the arguments of
the composed form are elementary forms, they are evaluated as described in
Chapter 7. If any of the arguments are themselves composed forms, the evaluation process recurs on these composed forms.

In greater detail, evaluation consists of evaluating all *args* of the composed
form, one at a time (generally from left to right), by the following steps:

1. If *args* is a constant, the constant is returned as the value of *args*.

2. If *args* is a variable, its binding is retrieved and returned as the
    value of *args*.

3. If *args* is a simple form, the value of the function of that form,
    applied to the values of its *parameters*, is returned as the value
    of *args*.

4. If *args* is a composed form, all partial results (i.e., the values of
    already evaluated *args*) are saved, and steps 1 through 5 are applied
    recursively to that *args*.

5. After all *args* are evaluated, the value of the function (i.e., *fname*),
    applied to the values of its arguments (i.e., all the *args*), is
    returned as the value of the composed form.

It is usually easier to evaluate composed forms than to understand the above
steps. Some examples should clear the air.

Examples:

$$(LAMBDA \ (J) \ (CONS \ (CAR \ J) \ (CAR \ (CDR \ J)))) \ ((A \ B))$$

By lambda conversion, lambda variable J is bound to the argument (A B), and
the composed form

$$(CONS \ (CAR \ J) \ (CAR \ (CDR \ J)))$$

is evaluated. This form has the syntax

$$(CONS \ arg_1 \ arg_2)$$

where arg_1 is the simple form (CAR J), and arg_2 is the composed form (CAR (CDR J)). Evaluating these arguments from left to right, we get

$$arg_1 = (CAR\ J) = A$$

But arg_2 is a composed form itself, with the syntax

$$(CAR\ arg_{21})$$

where arg_{21} is the simple form (CDR J).

To evaluate arg_2, we recur and first evaluate

$$arg_{21} = (CDR\ J) = (B)$$

Then, returning this value of the simple form arg_{21}, we get

$$arg_2 = (CAR\ arg_{21}) = B$$

Now, having evaluated all arguments of the composed form, we apply CONS to these arguments and yield

$$(CONS\ arg_1\ arg_2) = (A\ .\ B)$$

The value of the composed form, (A . B), is the value of the original lambda expression.

Consider another example:

$$(LAMBDA\ (X\ Y\ Z)\ (CONS\ X\ (CONS\ Y\ (CONS\ Z\ NIL))))\ (A\ B\ C)$$

By lambda conversion, X, Y, and Z are bound to A, B, and C, respectively. The composed form and its arguments have the syntax

$$(CONS\ X\ arg_1)$$
$$arg_1 = (CONS\ Y\ arg_{12})$$
$$arg_{12} = (CONS\ Z\ NIL)$$

Evaluation of these forms yields

$$\text{arg}_{12} = (\text{CONS Z NIL}) = (\text{C})$$
$$\text{arg}_1 = (\text{CONS Y arg}_{12}) = (\text{B C})$$
$$(\text{CONS X arg}_1) = (\text{A B C})$$

and the last value, (A B C), is the value of the lambda expression.

8.3   NESTED LAMBDA EXPRESSIONS

As we have seen, composed forms are generalizations of simple forms. By
examining the syntactic structures,

$$(\textit{fname parameters}) \qquad \text{simple form}$$

$$(\textit{fname args}) \qquad \text{composed form}$$

we see that the generalization is achieved by allowing any composed form, *args*,
to appear in lieu of any *parameter* of a simple form. The discussion of form
composition is not complete, however, until one further generalization is
considered: the generalization of *fname*.

Lambda expressions are functional expressions, and functional expressions may be
used wherever functions are acceptable. We have already observed this truth
in top-level function calls; e.g.,

$$\underbrace{\text{CAR}}_{s_1} \ \underbrace{((\text{A}))}_{s_2} = \text{A}$$

$$\underbrace{(\text{LAMBDA (J) (CAR J)})}_{s_1} \ \underbrace{((\text{A}))}_{s_2} = \text{A}$$

This truth holds equally well in composed forms. For this truth to be self
evident, consider the syntactic entity *fexp*, defined as either a function name,
i.e., *fname*, or a functional expression. Then the syntax of the most general
composed form is given by

$$(\textit{fexp args})$$

Examples:

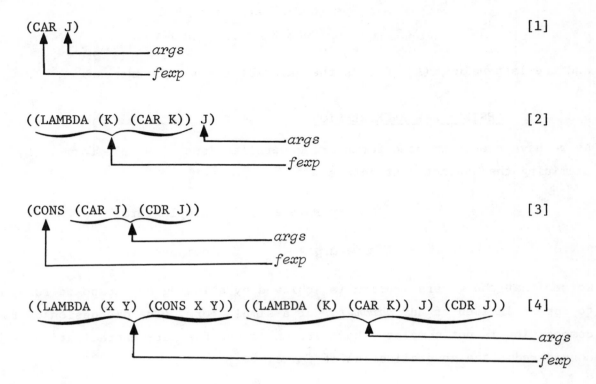

These four forms aptly demonstrate the complexity that is possible with form composition. Observe that forms [1] and [2] are semantically equivalent forms, as are forms [3] and [4]. Note further that form [4] is obtained from form [3] by substituting an equivalent lambda expression for CONS and by substituting form [2] for form [1].

In the spirit of generality of structures in LISP, forms may be composed with arbitrary complexity. In fact, by reason of constructs of the variety of form [4], it is theoretically possible to have an infinite number of semantically equivalent forms.

8.4   EVALUATING NESTED LAMBDA EXPRESSIONS

The rule for evaluating nested lambda expressions is exactly the same as that for evaluating composed forms given in Paragraph 8.2 (with one addition to step 5). Since we have generalized the syntax of composed forms as given in that paragraph, by replacing *fname* by *fexp*, step 5 should now read (with the addition underscored):

> "5. After all *args* are evaluated, the value of the
> function (i.e., *fexp*), applied to the values of its
> arguments (i.e., all the *args*), is returned as the
> value of the composed form. If *fexp* is a lambda
> expression, all lambda variables are bound by lambda
> conversion to the values of its arguments (i.e., all
> the *args*) and the value of the lambda form is the value
> of the composed form."

For compiler-based LISP systems, *fname* and *fexp* are treated nearly alike. If
fexp is a lambda expression, it is first compiled and then treated exactly as
fname. The difference lies between the name of a function and the explicit
definition of that function. Nested lambda expressions are analogous to "local
procedures" within an ALGOL procedure.

Examples:

If J is bound to (A B), then

$$(CAR\ J) = A \tag{1}$$
$$((LAMBDA\ (K)\ (CAR\ K))\ J) = A \tag{2}$$
$$((LAMBDA\ (K)\ (CAR\ K))\ (CDR\ J)) = B \tag{3}$$

In form [2], lambda variable K is bound to the value of J, i.e., (A B), by lambda
conversion. Then evaluating the simple form (CAR K), yields A. In form [3], K is
bound to the value of the simple form (CDR J), i.e., (B), by lambda conversion,
with the answer, B, resulting as the value of (CAR K).

$$\underbrace{(LAMBDA\ (J)\ ((LAMBDA\ (K)\ (CAR\ K))\ (CDR\ J)))}_{s_1}\ \underbrace{((A\ B))}_{s_2} = B \tag{4}$$

This top-level function call demonstrates how variable J might be bound for
form [3] above. It is, of course, bound by lambda conversion.

Evaluate the following:

1. (LAMBDA (A B) (CAR (CONS A B)))   (43 NUMBER)

2. (LAMBDA (A) (CAR (CDR A))) ((ARG LIST))

3. (LAMBDA (A) (CDR (CAR A))) (((A)))

4. (LAMBDA (A B) (CDR (CONS A B)))   (NUMBER 43)

5. (LAMBDA (B A) (CDR (CONS A B)))   (NUMBER 43)

6. (LAMBDA (A B) (CAR (CDR (CONS A B))))   (A (Y))

7. (LAMBDA (J) (CONS (CONS J NIL) NIL)) ((LIST))

8. (LAMBDA (J) (CAR (CAR (CONS (CDR J) (CDR J))))) ((A B))

9. (LAMBDA (J) (CAR (CONS 123Q3 J))) (NIL)

10. (LAMBDA (J) (CONS (CAR J) (CDR J))) ((A . B))

Note that problem 10 clearly demonstrates the relationship between CAR, CDR, and CONS.

11. CAR could be called FIRST since it finds the first element of a list.
    Write a lambda expression (using only CAR and CDR) by composition of
    forms which finds the third element of a list.

For the argument

            ((A B C) D)

compose and evaluate your own lambda expressions (using only CAR and CDR)
that evaluate exactly as the following abbreviations (see Paragraph 5.5).

12. CAAR

13. CADR

14. CDAR

15. CADAR

Evaluate the following:

16. (LAMBDA (U V) ((LAMBDA (X Y) (CONS (CAR X) (CDR Y))) U V)) ((A) (B C))

17. (LAMBDA (U V) ((LAMBDA (X Y) (CONS (CAR X) Y)) U (CDR V))) ((A) (B C))

18. (LAMBDA (W X) (CAR ((LAMBDA (Y Z) (CONS Y Z)) W X))) ((A) (B C))

19. (LAMBDA (W X) (CDR ((LAMBDA (Y Z) (CONS Y Z)) (CAR W) (CDR X)))) ((A) (B C))
20. (LAMBDA (J) (CONS

           ((LAMBDA (X Y) (CONS Y (CONS X NIL))) (CAR J) (CADR J))

           ((LAMBDA (U V) (CONS (CONS V (CONS U NIL)) NIL)) (CADDR J) (CADDDR J))
       )) ((A B C D))

CHAPTER 9.
SPECIAL FORMS

In LISP, there exists a collection of built-in forms that superficially look like functions. They are called *special forms*, and are treated differently than are functions. When they appear in the *fexp* position of a form, that form is evaluated in a special manner; the manner of evaluation depends upon the given special form. In general, special forms fall into two classes:

1. Special forms with an indefinite number of arguments.

2. Special forms that wish their arguments unevaluated so that they may control the way their arguments are evaluated.

Some special forms, such as AND and OR (see Chapter 12) reside in both classes.

Each special form must be studied in detail to determine its rules of evaluation. One such special form, LAMBDA, we have already learned how to evaluate. Many of the remaining chapters are devoted to similar examination. In this chapter, we shall consider a few important special forms which belong to these two classes.

9.1   LIST

LIST, the first special form we shall consider, has an indefinite number of arguments. These arguments may be any form, i.e., elementary, composed, or special. The arguments are evaluated; the value of LIST is a list of the values of these arguments. It may be defined by the following identities:

```
(LIST)             =  NIL
(LIST A1)          =  (CONS A1 NIL)
(LIST A1 A2)       =  (CONS A1 (CONS A2 NIL))
      .                        .
      .                        .
      .                        .
(LIST A1 A2 ... AN) = (CONS A1 (CONS A2 (CONS ... (CONS AN NIL) ... )))
```

<u>Examples</u>:

```
(LIST 1 2)  =  (1 2)
(CONS 1 2)  =  (1 . 2)
(LIST T NIL 35)  =  (T NIL 35)
(LIST T (LIST NIL (LIST 35)))  =  (T (NIL (35)))
(LAMBDA (X Y) (LIST (CONS X Y) (LIST X Y))) (A B) = ((A . B) (A B))
```

9.2   <u>QUOTE</u>

QUOTE is a special form that wishes to receive its single argument unevaluated. The argument may be any S-expression. QUOTE returns the S-expression, still unevaluated, as its value.

The syntax of QUOTE is given by

(QUOTE e)

where e may be any S-expression.

Consider the following two examples:

(LAMBDA (X) (CAR X)) ((A B C)) = A

(LAMBDA (X) (QUOTE X)) ((A B C)) = X

In both examples, the variable X is bound to the list (A B C) by lambda conversion. In the first example, the form

(CAR X)

is evaluated by first evaluating the variable X and then applying the function CAR to that value. In the second example, however, we see the suppression of evaluation yielded by QUOTE. The form

(QUOTE X)

is evaluated by simply returning the argument X. We do not evaluate X as we did in the first example. We speak of X as being *quoted*.

<u>Examples</u>:

                  (LAMBDA NIL (QUOTE ALPHA)) ( )

evaluates to ALPHA.

                  (LAMBDA (X) (CONS (QUOTE ALPHA) X)) (BETA)

evaluates to (ALPHA . BETA).

                  (LAMBDA (J) (CONS (QUOTE J) J)) (FOO)

evaluates to (J . FOO).

Since arbitrary S-expressions in LISP may look like forms, QUOTE must be used
to represent symbolic constants as data of forms. Otherwise, an attempt will
be made to evaluate the data as a form--a situation that usually results in
an error. For example, the form

                  (CAR (1 2 3))

will yield an error, since the list, (1 2 3), is not quoted and obviously cannot be evaluated as a meaningful form. The correct form should be

                  (CAR (QUOTE (1 2 3))) = 1

9.3   <u>EVALQUOTE</u>

In Chapter 5 we introduced the syntax for communicating with the LISP supervisor.
We shall now examine this communication more closely and see that it is a method
of passing a pair of unevaluated arguments to a special form, called EVALQUOTE.
The reader is cautioned that the treatment given here for EVALQUOTE is pedagogical
and not the actual way it is implemented in most systems, though the effect is
the same.

Consider the following form:

                  (CONS (QUOTE CONS) (QUOTE (T NIL)))   [1]

When evaluated, the form yields a value

                  (CONS T NIL)   [2]

-60-

which is itself a legal form. If we evaluate form [2], we get

$$(T . NIL) = (T)$$

But, form [2] is the value of form [1], i.e., it is data, and LISP evaluates a form only once. To evaluate form [2] would, in effect, be evaluating form [1] twice. How then do we evaluate a computed form? EVAL to the rescue!

Let us assume there exists a primitive system function, called EVAL, that takes one argument, the value of which must be a form. EVAL will simply evaluate that form and return the value. (This EVAL may differ slightly from that available in a given LISP implementation.)

The syntax of EVAL is given by

$$(EVAL e)$$

where e must evaluate to a form.

For example, the composed form

$$(EVAL (QUOTE (CONS T NIL)))$$

has the structure

$$(EVAL e)$$

where

$$e = (QUOTE (CONS T NIL))$$

The value of e is (CONS T NIL), a simple form. It is this value to which EVAL is applied, yielding the value (T).

It is interesting to note that the value of form [1] above is exactly the value of e in this example. Hence, the value of

$$(EVAL (CONS (QUOTE CONS) (QUOTE (T NIL))))$$

is also (T).

With EVAL now defined, let us examine EVALQUOTE.

As we saw earlier, the pair of S-expressions to the supervisor (which we called s_1 and s_2 previously) consists of a functional expression, or function name, s_1, and a list of arguments, s_2, for s_1. For example,

$$\underbrace{\text{CONS}}_{s_1} \quad \underbrace{\text{(A B)}}_{s_2}$$

Consider the general top-level pair of S-expressions for the supervisor as

$$\underbrace{f_n}_{s_1} \quad \underbrace{(\text{arg}_1 \ \text{arg}_2 \ \dots \ \text{arg}_n)}_{s_2}$$

The manner in which the supervisor evaluates this pair can be explained by considering the evaluation of the following form:

$$(\text{EVAL E})$$

where the <u>binding</u> of E is given as

$$E = (f_n \ (\text{QUOTE arg}_1) \ (\text{QUOTE arg}_2) \ \dots \ (\text{QUOTE arg}_n))$$

To evaluate this form, the variable E is evaluated yielding the value

$$(f_n \ (\text{QUOTE arg}_1) \ (\text{QUOTE arg}_2) \ \dots \ (\text{QUOTE arg}_n))$$

It is this value to which EVAL is applied. The final value, then, is the function f_n applied to the <u>values</u> of its arguments. Since the arguments of f_n are quoted constants that evaluate to themselves, the final value of (EVAL E) is the value of f_n applied to arg_1, arg_2, $\dots$, arg_n--exactly the result we desire.

The important role played by the function EVAL and the special form QUOTE in the operation of the supervisor leads to the name EVALQUOTE. Indeed, most LISP supervisors are EVALQUOTE supervisors.

To illustrate the EVALQUOTE process more clearly, let us step through the process once again, but with the EVALQUOTE pair

$$\underbrace{\text{CONS}}_{s_1} \; \underbrace{\text{(A B)}}_{s_2}$$

We are to evaluate the form

$$(\text{EVAL E})$$

where the binding of E is

$$E = (f_n \; (\text{QUOTE } arg_1) \; (\text{QUOTE } arg_2) \; ... \; (\text{QUOTE } arg_n))$$

For this EVALQUOTE pair, f_n is CONS, arg_1 is A, and arg_2 is B. Therefore, the binding of E is the form

$$(\text{CONS (QUOTE A) (QUOTE B)}) \qquad\qquad [3]$$

The value, then, of (EVAL E) is (A . B), which is the value of form [3]. Another way of stating it is this: (EVAL E) is the _double_ evaluation of E.

The behavior of the EVALQUOTE supervisor should be more understandable now that we have "peeked" behind the scenes. EVALQUOTE _quotes each argument_ in the list, s_2, before it applies the function, s_1. This explains why it is proper to enter the pair

$$\text{CONS (A B)}$$

at the top level, and necessary to write

$$(\text{CONS (QUOTE A) (QUOTE B)})$$

as an equivalent form at all other levels. EVALQUOTE is a programming convenience that does our quoting for us.

In Chapter 17 we shall review the above and actually define EVALQUOTE as a LISP special form. We cannot do so now as we have not as yet acquired the recursive or iterative programming skills necessary to construct the binding of E.

9.4   <u>EXERCISES</u>

Evaluate:

1.   (LAMBDA NIL (QUOTE X)) ( )

2.   (LAMBDA (J) (QUOTE J)) (ALPHA)

3.   (LAMBDA (J) (QUOTE (AN S EXPRESSION))) (ALPHA)

4.   (LAMBDA (J) (CAR (QUOTE (A B C)))) (ALPHA)

5.   (LAMBDA (J) (CDR (QUOTE (J J)))) (NOTJ)

6.   (LAMBDA (A B) (CONS A B)) (QUOTE EXPR)

7.   (LAMBDA (A B) (CAR (CONS (QUOTE A) B)))   (ALPHA BETA)

8.   (LAMBDA NIL (QUOTE

        (NOW IS THE TIME FOR ALL GOOD MEN TO COME TO

        THE AID OF THE PARTY))) ( )

9.   (LAMBDA NIL (CONS (QUOTE A) (QUOTE B))) ( )

10. (LAMBDA NIL (QUOTE

        (LAMBDA (X) X))) ( )

11. (LAMBDA (A B C) (LIST A B C)) (ONE TWO THREE)

12. (LAMBDA (A B C) (CONS A (CONS B (CONS C NIL)))) (ONE TWO THREE)

13. (LAMBDA (A B C) (LIST NIL A NIL B NIL C)) (F F F)

14. (LAMBDA (A B C) (LIST (QUOTE F) A (QUOTE F) B (QUOTE F) C)) (F F F)

15. (LAMBDA (A B C D) (LIST (LIST NIL (QUOTE F) A)

                            (LIST T (QUOTE T) B)

                            (LIST NIL (QUOTE NIL) C)

                            (LIST 123 (QUOTE 123) D))) (F T NIL 123)

16. EVAL ((QUOTE X))

17. EVAL ((QUOTE J))

18. EVAL ((QUOTE (AN S EXPRESSION)))

19. EVAL ((CAR (QUOTE (A B C))))

20. EVAL ((CDR (QUOTE (J J))))

Compare your answers for problems 1-5 and 16-20.

21. (LAMBDA (J) (EVAL J)) ((QUOTE ABLE))

22. (LAMBDA (J) (CONS (EVAL J) J)) ((QUOTE ABLE))

23. (LAMBDA (J K) (EVAL (LIST J K))) (CAR (QUOTE (ABLE)))

24. (LAMBDA (J K) (CONS (EVAL J) (EVAL K))) ((CAR (QUOTE (CONS))) (LIST A B))
25. (LAMBDA (J) (EVAL (LIST (QUOTE CDR)

                      (LIST (QUOTE QUOTE) (EVAL J))))) ((QUOTE (A B)))

CHAPTER 10.
DEFINE

Evaluating lambda expressions at the top level is a one-shot proposition. If we wish to evaluate the same expression for different arguments, we must enter the entire doublet again. After evaluation, the state of the LISP system is as it was prior to execution. This is desirable for many situations, including debugging, code execution, and program formulation. However, for the majority of cases, we would like to save the expression as part of the LISP system, give it a function name, and use it repeatedly to build larger programs. We can do this with the *pseudo-function* DEFINE.

Pseudo-functions are expressions that are used like functions, but for their effect rather than for their value. They have "side effects" of interest, but effects not reflected in the value of the expression. Input-output functions are other examples of pseudo-functions.

10.1   DEFINE SYNTAX

DEFINE is a pseudo-function that takes <u>one</u> argument, a list of functions to be defined. Like CAR, CDR, and all other single-argument functions evaluated at the top level, the general syntax is:

$$\text{DEFINE}\ (\ e_1\ )$$

where the argument, e, is a list of functions to be defined.

The format of e is:

$$_2(f_1\ f_2\ f_3\ \cdots\ f_n)_2$$

where the f_i are the definitions for the functions we wish to define. The formats are all the same, namely a lambda expression, prefixed with a name. This name, a literal atom, will become the function name. Thus

$$_3(\text{name}\ _4(\text{LAMBDA}\ \textit{varlist body})_{43})$$

-66-

is the general syntax for any of the f_i function definitions, and

```
        DEFINE ((
              12

                    (name  (LAMBDA varlist body))
                        1
                     3     4                  43


                    (name  (LAMBDA varlist body))
                        2
                     3     4                  43
                        .
                        .
                        .

                    (name  (LAMBDA varlist body))
                        n
                     3     4                  43
              ))
              21
```

is the general syntax for the complete DEFINE expression.

Note the parentheses, their depth and meaning. The No. 1 pair delimits the second S-expression, s_2, for EVALQUOTE; pair No. 2 delimits the single argument of DEFINE as a list; the No. 3 pairs delimit each of the n functional expressions to be defined.

Example:

```
        DEFINE ((
              12

                    (THIRD (LAMBDA (X) (CAR (CDR (CDR X)))))
                     3     4     5 5 5  6   7   76543

                    (IN3 (LAMBDA (X) (CAR (CAR (CAR X)))))
                     3   4     5 5 5  6   7   76543

                    (SECONDOF1ST (LAMBDA (X) (CAR (CDR (CAR X)))))
                     3           4     5 5 5  6   7   76543

              ))
              21
```

If we wish to define only one function, the syntax is still the same, with the argument list of DEFINE containing one functional expression.

-67-

10.2 EVALUATING DEFINE

The value of the pseudo-function DEFINE is a list of the names of the functions defined. For the example above, LISP would return

$$\text{(THIRD IN3 SECONDOF1ST)}$$

What have we really done by evaluating DEFINE? For a compiler-based LISP system, we have compiled machine code for each of the functional expressions in the argument list. This machine code becomes a permanent part of the LISP system, which can be referenced by the name given in the functional expression, and can be used to evaluate data like all other system functions. For interpretive LISP systems, the functional expression defines the function, and the expression is retained by the system for recall and interpretation when the function is called.

10.3 REDEFINING

If, after defining a function, you find the definition to be in error or you wish to change the function's definition (i.e., change the function's lambda expression) for other reasons, you need only use DEFINE again with the old function name and a new lambda expression. The new lambda expression will be compiled and referenced under the old name. The old compiled code is discarded and cannot be referenced again. As with list structure that is discarded and collected later, discarded compiled code may be collected later. The general problem of internal storage management in LISP systems is handled by a program called the "garbage collector". In some LISP systems, the space occupied by the old code cannot be reclaimed and is lost to the system. Repeated redefinitions build up such "garbage" and should be avoided.

Feel free to redefine programs at will. If you try various definitions on an actual computer, be careful not to define programs whose names are system functions, as you will redefine functions possibly used internally by the system and thereby get into trouble. A representative set of system function names to be avoided is listed on the inside front and back covers of this book.

10.4   <u>EXERCISES</u>

Define the following new functions and test them on list (A B C D E)

1. (FIRST (LAMBDA (X) (CAR X)))
2. (SECOND (LAMBDA (Y) (CADR Y)))
3. (THIRD (LAMBDA (Z) (CAR (CDDR Z))))
4. CADDDDR
5. Define a function, called REVDOT, that reverses the CAR and CDR of any dotted pair. Try it on the following arguments:

        (A . B)
        ((A) . (B))
        (((FIRST)) . (LAST))

CHAPTER 11.
CONDITIONAL EXPRESSIONS

The class of functions that can be formed with what we know so far is quite
limited and not very interesting. We need functions that branch conditionally
on the value of forms and thereby allow a much larger class of functions to be
defined. The special form COND accepts an indefinite number of arguments and
conditionally evaluates these arguments based upon their values. COND thus
allows us to perform analysis of differing cases.

11.1   SYNTAX OF CONDITIONAL EXPRESSIONS

A *conditional expression* is a special form in LISP and has the following syntax:

$$(COND \ (p_1 \ e_1) \ (p_2 \ e_2) \ ... \ (p_n \ e_n))$$

where the p_i are forms that evaluate to NIL or not NIL, and the e_i are forms
that can have any desired value.

COND takes an indefinite number of arguments, called *clauses*, each of which is
a list containing a p_i and its corresponding e_1. It accepts all its arguments
unevaluated; as a special form, it evaluates these arguments from left to right
under strict control as described below.

11.2   EVALUATING CONDITIONAL EXPRESSIONS

LISP evaluates the arguments of a conditional expression from left to right as
follows:

> If the value of p_1 is not NIL,
>   then the value of COND is the value of e_1; else,
> If the value of p_2 is not NIL,
>   then the value of COND is the value of e_2; else,
> If the value of p_3 is not NIL, etc.

The entire expression is searched by evaluating the p_i of each clause, until the first p_i that is not NIL is found, and then the corresponding e_i of that clause is evaluated. Note that e_i is never evaluated if the corresponding p_i of that clause is NIL.

If a non-NIL clause cannot be found (i.e., all p_i are NIL), then the value of the entire expression is undefined. To protect against this occurrence, LISP programmers usually set the p_n of the last clause equal to T and set the last expression, e_n of that clause, equal to some terminating expression. Since T is a symbolic constant, it always evaluates non-NIL and COND is always defined. If nothing else proves non-NIL, then the value of e_n will be the value of the conditional expression. In some LISP systems, an undefined conditional expression usually results in an error during evaluation of the expression. On other LISP systems, an undefined conditional expression returns a value of NIL.

Examples:

1. The function NOT returns as its value the negation of its single argument. If its argument is NIL, it returns not NIL, i.e., T. If its argument is not NIL, it returns NIL. It can be defined in LISP as follows:

    DEFINE (((NOT (LAMBDA (J) (COND (J NIL) (T T))))))

2. Using NOT, we can define the function LN that "counts" the length of a list. It returns either 0, 1, 2, or LOTS--depending on whether there are none (empty list), one, two, three or more elements of the list, respectively. For example,

    DEFINE (((LN (LAMBDA (L)
        (COND ((NOT L) 0)
            ((NOT (CDR L)) 1)
            ((NOT (CDDR L)) 2)
            (T (QUOTE LOTS))))))))

3. The propositional connective "implies" has the following truth table:

X	Y	X → Y
true	true	true
true	false	false
false	true	true
false	false	true

If we let T and NIL represent true and false, respectively, using COND, we can define IMPLIES in two ways:

DEFINE (((IMPLIES (LAMBDA (X Y) (COND (X Y) (T T))))))

DEFINE (((IMPLIES (LAMBDA (X Y) (COND (X (COND (Y T) (T NIL)))
(T T))))))

The second definition demonstrates the nesting of conditionals; however, the first definition is more elegant, since it takes full advantage of the nature of the data by letting the variables act as forms.

11.3   SELECT

The special form SELECT is a more general conditional form. In most LISP systems, SELECT is used as a "switch" to control program flow, while COND is used as described above.

SELECT has the syntax

$$(\text{SELECT } p \ (p_1 \ e_1) \ (p_2 \ e_2) \ \cdots \ (p_n \ e_n) \ e)$$

where the p_i are evaluated in sequence from left to right until one is found that is equal to p.

Then the value of SELECT is the value of the corresponding e_i. If no such p_i is found, the value of SELECT is that of e.

The LISP function IMPLIES can be written using SELECT. Compare this definition with those of Paragraph 11.2.

DEFINE (((IMPLIES (LAMBDA (X Y) (SELECT X (Y T) Y)))))

11.4   <u>EXERCISES</u>

Evaluate the following:

1. (LAMBDA NIL (COND (NIL (QUOTE FALSE)) (T (QUOTE TRUE)))) ( )
2. (LAMBDA (A B C) (COND (T A) (T B) (T C))) (1 2 3)
3. (LAMBDA (A B C) (COND (NIL A) (NIL B) (NIL C))) (1 2 3)
4. (LAMBDA (J) (CONS J (COND (J NIL) (T J)))) (T)
5. (LAMBDA (J K) (SELECT J ((QUOTE ODD) (CAR K))
                       ((QUOTE EVEN) (CDR K))
                       (QUOTE NOP))) (2 (1 2))

6. Define the function OR2 (X Y) that returns NIL as its value if both X and Y are NIL, and returns T otherwise.

7. Define the function XOR2 (X Y) that returns T as its value if X or Y are non-NIL, but not both, and returns NIL otherwise.

8. Define the function AND2 (X Y) that returns T as its value if X and Y are both non-NIL, and returns NIL otherwise.

9. For the COND expression

$$(COND \ (p_1 \ e_1) \ (p_2 \ e_2) \ ... \ (p_n \ e_n))$$

give an equivalent expression using only SELECT.

10. For the SELECT expression

$$(SELECT \ p \ (p_1 \ e_1) \ (p_2 \ e_2) \ ... \ (p_n \ e_n) \ e)$$

give an equivalent expression using COND. Assume there exists a function EQUAL (X Y) that returns T if X and Y are the same S-expression.

CHAPTER 12.
PREDICATE FUNCTIONS

To perform interesting computations with conditional forms, we need a variety of functions that test data to determine if a datum is a number, an empty list, an atom, equal to some other datum, less than or greater than some other number, a member of a list, etc.

The LISP world is divided on this matter into two camps: purists and pragmatists. Purists call the test functions *predicates*, and require such functions to return one of two values--true or false. The pragmatist argues that conditional forms, as implemented on all LISP systems, test only for NIL. He, like the purist, defines a predicate as a function that returns either T (true) or NIL (false). However, he postulates that an additional class of functions exist that may have NIL as but one value in an infinite domain of non-NIL values. Since NIL is half the domain of predicate functions, these functions are called *semi-predicates* and may be used in the predicate position of conditional expressions, e.g., the p_i of a COND clause. CDR is a perfect example of a semi-predicate.

This chapter examines a number of predicates built into most LISP systems.

12.1   ATOM

The predicate ATOM has <u>one</u> argument. The value of ATOM is T if the value of the argument is an atomic symbol; otherwise, the value of ATOM is NIL.

<u>Examples</u>:

```
(ATOM T) = T
(ATOM 1.23) = T
(ATOM NIL) = T
(ATOM (QUOTE AVERYLONGSTRINGOFLETTERS)) = T
(ATOM (QUOTE (A B C))) = NIL
(ATOM (CONS T NIL)) = NIL
(ATOM (CDR (QUOTE (A)))) = T
```

12.2   EQ

Note:

> The predicate EQ is very implementation-dependent,
> based upon the canonical form of structures inter-
> nally used by a given LISP system. You are therefore
> advised to consult your own particular reference
> literature.

EQ is a predicate that has two arguments. The value of EQ is T if the values of the arguments are the same pointer, i.e., the same internal address; other-wise, the value of EQ is NIL. In all LISP implementations, literal atoms have unique internal addresses, therefore, EQ will be T if the values of the argu-ments are the same literal atom.

In some recently developed systems, small numbers (e.g., 0 to 1000) are also unique and can be successfully tested with EQ. Also, some systems store list structure uniquely, and for these systems EQ can compare two equivalent lists.

For purposes of this text, we shall assume EQ behaves according to more conven-tional systems and can only test literal atoms successfully.

Examples:

        (EQ T T) = T
        (EQ T NIL) = NIL
        (EQ ( ) NIL) = T
        (EQ (QUOTE A) (QUOTE B)) = NIL
        (EQ (ATOM (QUOTE B)) T) = T

12.3   EQUAL

The predicate EQUAL takes two arguments. The value of EQUAL is T if the values of its arguments are identical S-expressions; otherwise, the value of EQUAL is NIL. EQUAL may be used to test the equality of numbers, literal atoms, and list structures. It is more general than EQ, but commensurately more time-consuming in its operation.

Examples:

$$(EQUAL\ T\ T) = T$$
$$(EQUAL\ NIL\ NIL) = T$$
$$(EQUAL\ 1.23\ 1.23) = T$$
$$(EQUAL\ (QUOTE\ (A\ B\ ))\ (QUOTE\ (A\ B))) = T$$
$$(EQUAL\ (LIST\ T)\ T) = NIL$$
$$(EQUAL\ 17Q\ 15) = T$$

Note:

        EQUAL will accept and convert numbers of differing
types before it performs the test for equality.
For the case of floating-point numbers, they must
agree within a specified accuracy that is dependent
upon the capacity of the machine.

12.4 ARITHMETIC PREDICATES

All of the following predicates end with the letter "P", for "predicate", as a
mnemonic aid. Their arguments must evaluate to numbers, or else they are
undefined.

(NUMBERP N)   = T if N evaluates to a number of any type

                        = NIL if N evaluates to a non-atomic S-expression

                        = NIL if N evaluates to a literal atom

(FIXP N)   = T if N evaluates to an integer or octal number

                        = NIL if N evaluates to a floating-point number

                        = Undefined if N evaluates to a non-numeric S-expression

(FLOATP N)   = T if N evaluates to a floating-point number

                        = NIL if N evaluates to an integer or octal number

                        = Undefined if N evaluates to a non-numeric S-expression

(ZEROP N)   = T if N evaluates to zero of any numeric type

                        = NIL if N evaluates to a non-zero number

                        = Undefined if N evaluates to a non-numeric S-expression

```
(ONEP N)            =  T if N evaluates to one of any numeric type

                    =  NIL if N evaluates to a number other than one

                    =  Undefined if N evaluates to a non-numeric S-expression


(MINUSP N)          =  T if N evaluates to a negative number of any numeric type

                    =  NIL if N evaluates to a positive number

                    =  Undefined if N evaluates to a non-numeric S-expression


(GREATERP N1 N2)    =  T if the value of N1 is greater than the value of N2,
                       where N1 and N2 may be any numeric types

                    =  NIL if the value of N1 is less than or equal to the
                       value of N2

                    =  Undefined if N1 or N2 evaluates to a non-numeric S-expression


(EVENP N)           =  T if N evaluates to an even number of any numeric type

                    =  NIL if N evaluates to an odd number

                    =  Undefined if N evaluates to a non-numeric S-expression


(LESSP N1 N2)       =  T if the value of N1 is less than the value of N2,
                       where N1 and N2 may be any numeric types

                    =  NIL if the value of N1 is greater than or equal to the
                       value of N2

                    =  Undefined if N1 or N2 evaluates to a non-numeric S-expression
```

12.5   LIST PREDICATES

```
(NULL L)            =  T if the value of L is the empty list ( ) or NIL

                    =  NIL if the value of L is not NIL or ( )


(MEMBER L1 L2)      =  T if the value of L1 is a top-level element of a list
                       returned as the value of L2

                    =  NIL if the value of L1 is not an element of the value of L2

                    =  NIL if the value of L1 is an element of a sublist of the
                       value of L2; e.g.,


                       (MEMBER (QUOTE A) (QUOTE ((A)) )) = NIL
```

Note:

> If the definition of MEMBER uses EQ rather than
> EQUAL, the value of L1 must be a literal atom
> if MEMBER is ever to return T. If EQUAL is used,
> the value of L1 may be any S-expression.

12.6   LOGICAL CONNECTIVES

(NOT P)   = T if P evaluates to NIL

                           = NIL if P evaluates to any non-NIL S-expression

Note:

> NOT and NULL are synonymous functions.

(AND x_1 x_2 ... x_n)   = T if the values of all x_i are non-NIL

                           = NIL if the value of any x_i is NIL

Note:

> AND is a special form and takes an indefinite
> number of arguments, not a list of arguments. The
> arguments of AND are evaluated in sequence from left
> to right, until one is found that is false, or until
> the end of the list is reached. The value of AND is
> T if all arguments are non-NIL. The value of AND is
> NIL if any argument is NIL; the remaining arguments
> are unevaluated. Also,
>
> (AND) = T

(OR x_1 x_2 ... x_n)   = T if the value of any x_i is non-NIL

                           = NIL if the values of all x_i are NIL

Note:

OR is a special form and takes an indefinite number
of arguments, not a list of arguments. The arguments of OR are evaluated in sequence from left to
right, until one is found that is non-NIL, or until
the end of the list is reached. The value of OR is
T if any argument is non-NIL; the remaining arguments are unevaluated. The value of OR is NIL if
all arguments are NIL. Also,

(OR) = NIL

12.7   EXERCISES

Evaluate these pairs for EVALQUOTE:

1.   (LAMBDA (J) (CONS (EQ J J) (QUOTE (F T F)))) (X)
2.   ATOM (NIL)
3.   NULL (NIL)
4.   NULL ((NIL))
5.   NULL (( ))
6.   EQUAL (0 NIL)
7.   NUMBERP (1965)
8.   NUMBERP ((1965))
9.   (LAMBDA (A B C) (OR (ZEROP A)
                        (FIXP B)
                        (FLOATP C))) (1 2 3)
10.   (LAMBDA (J) (NOT (AND (ATOM J)
                        (NUMBERP J)
                        (FLOATP J)
                        (MINUSP J)
                        (NOT (ZEROP J))))) (-1.0)
11.   GREATERP (1964 1965)
12.   GREATERP (1965 1964)
13.   LESSP (10Q 10)
14.   MEMBER (HEAR (NOW HEAR THIS))

15. MEMBER (HEAR (NOW (HEAR THIS)))

16. (LAMBDA (J) (OR (ONEP J) (EVENP J))) (2.0)

17. The propositional connective "equivalent" has the following truth table:

X	Y	X EQUIV Y
true	true	true
true	false	false
false	true	false
false	false	true

If T and NIL represent true and false, respectively, define the LISP function EQUIV using only predicates. Test it on the following EVALQUOTE pairs:

```
EQUIV (T T) = T
EQUIV (T NIL) = NIL
EQUIV (NIL T) = NIL
EQUIV (NIL NIL) = T
```

18. The propositional connective "implies" has the following truth table:

X	Y	X → Y
true	true	true
true	false	false
false	true	true
false	false	true

If T and NIL represent true and false, respectively, define the LISP function IMPLIES using only predicates. Test it on the following EVALQUOTE pairs:

```
IMPLIES (T T) = T
IMPLIES (T NIL) = NIL
IMPLIES (NIL T) = T
IMPLIES (NIL NIL) = T
```

19. Define the predicate INSEQ that is T if a list of 5 elements are all numbers in ascending or descending order and NIL otherwise. Do not use COND; use nested lambda expressions. Test it with these EVALQUOTE pairs:

$$INSEQ~((1~2~3~4~5)) = T$$
$$INSEQ~((5~4~3~2~1)) = T$$
$$INSEQ~((1Q~2.0~99~1000Q~1000.0)) = T$$
$$INSEQ~((10Q~10~10.0~11.0~12Q)) = NIL$$
$$INSEQ~((10~9~8~7Q~7)) = NIL$$

20. Given the function DIFFERENCE that yields the difference of two numbers, define the predicate EQN that is T if its two arguments are the identical atom and NIL otherwise. Do not use EQUAL. Test it with these EVALQUOTE pairs:

$$EQN~(A~A) = T$$
$$EQN~(1~1.0) = NIL$$
$$EQN~(77Q~77Q) = T$$
$$EQN~((A)~A) = NIL$$

CHAPTER 13.
ARITHMETIC FUNCTIONS

Chapter 4 discusses the LISP syntax of numbers; it might pay to review that chapter. Let us review three important points:

1. Numbers may occur in S-expressions because they are atomic symbols.

2. Numbers are constants. They do not need to be quoted.

3. Numbers should not be used as variables or function names, e.g., never in the *varlist* of a lambda expression.

13.1   GENERAL COMMENTS

All the arithmetic functions must be given numbers as arguments, or S-expressions that evaluate to numbers; otherwise an error condition will result for most implementations of LISP.

The numerical arguments to arithmetic functions may be any type of number, i.e., integer, octal, or floating-point. An arithmetic function may be given some fixed-point (i.e., integer or octal) and some floating-point arguments at the same time. If all of the arguments for a function are fixed-point numbers, then the value will be a fixed-point number. (Integer and octal arguments always yield an integer value.) If at least one argument is a floating-point number, then the value of that function will be a floating-point number.

13.2   LISP ARITHMETIC FUNCTIONS

In much of the published LISP literature, functions are presented as top-level calls to EVALQUOTE, as this style is analogous to mathematical convention. I have avoided that style until now as it confuses the issue of variables and constants, particularly since EVALQUOTE quotes its arguments. By writing functions as simple forms, we know that the arguments of the form are evaluated before the function is applied. For example, the atoms A and B are constants in the top-level expression

CONS (A B)

whereas A and B are variables in the simple form

$$(CONS \ A \ B)$$

With the introduction of arithmetic functions below, we have the opportunity to adopt the more conventional style; we cannot confuse the "pedagogic variables" of definition with the numbers actually required by the functions.

$$PLUS \ (x_1 \ x_2 \ \dots \ x_n) = x_1 + x_2 + \dots + x_n$$

PLUS is a special form of an indefinite number of arguments, the value of which is the algebraic sum of the arguments.

$$DIFFERENCE \ (x \ y) = x - y$$

DIFFERENCE has for its value the algebraic difference of its arguments.

$$MINUS \ (x) = -x$$

MINUS has for its value the negative of its argument.

$$TIMES \ (x_1 \ x_2 \ \dots \ x_n) = x_1 * x_2 * \dots * x_n$$

TIMES is a special form of an indefinite number of arguments, the value of which is the product (with correct sign) of its arguments.

$$ADD1 \ (x) = x + 1$$

ADD1 adds one to its argument and returns the sum as its value. The value is fixed-point or floating-point according to the argument type.

$$SUB1 \ (x) = x - 1$$

SUB1 subtracts one from its argument and returns the difference as its value. The value is fixed-point or floating-point according to the argument type.

$$\text{MAX } (x_1 \ x_2 \ \ldots \ x_n)$$

MAX chooses the largest of its arguments for its value. Note that

$$\text{MAX } (3 \ 1Q \ 2.0) = 3.0$$

yields a floating-point number, since at least one argument was floating-point.

$$\text{MIN } (x_1 \ x_2 \ \ldots \ x_n)$$

MIN chooses the smallest of its arguments for its value.

$$\text{QUOTIENT } (x \ y) = x \ / \ y$$

QUOTIENT computes the quotient of its arguments. For fixed-point arguments, the value is the number-theoretic quotient, e.g., QUOTIENT (5 2) = 2. An out-of-range result will cause a LISP error.

$$\text{REMAINDER } (x \ y)$$

REMAINDER computes the number-theoretic remainder for fixed-point arguments (e.g., REMAINDER (5 2) = 1), and the floating-point residue for floating-point arguments.

$$\text{DIVIDE } (x \ y)$$

DIVIDE returns as its value a list of the QUOTIENT and the REAMINDER of its arguments. It could be defined by:

$$\text{(DIVIDE (LAMBDA (X Y) (LIST (QUOTIENT X Y) (REMAINDER X Y))))}$$

$$\text{EXPT } (x \ y) = x^y$$

If both x and y are fixed-point numbers, x^y is computed by iterative multiplication. Otherwise, the yth power of x is computed by using logarithms. The first argument, x, cannot be negative if y is not an integer.

$$\text{SQRT } (x) = \sqrt{|x|}$$

SQRT is a LISP function, the value of which is the square root of the absolute value of the argument. The value is always given as a floating-point number.

$$\text{RECIP } (x) = 1 \; / \; x$$

RECIP computes and returns as its value the reciprocal of its argument. The reciprocal of any fixed-point number is defined to be zero.

$$\text{ABSVAL } (x) = \mid x \mid$$

ABSVAL returns as its value the absolute value of its argument. If x is positive, it returns x. If x is negative, it returns the value of MINUS(x).

$$\text{FLOAT } (x)$$

FLOAT is a LISP function, the value of which is the floating-point equivalent of its argument. It could be defined by:

(FLOAT (LAMBDA (X) (PLUS X 0.0)))

$$\text{ENTIER } (x)$$

ENTIER is a LISP function, the value of which, for positive numbers, is the largest integer less than or equal to its argument. For negative numbers it is MINUS the ENTIER of the magnitude of the argument. For example:

ENTIER (93.75) = 93
ENTIER (-3.75) = -3
ENTIER (0.35) = 0
ENTIER (-0.35) = 0

Whereas FLOAT converts a fixed-point number to a floating-point number, ENTIER converts a floating-point number to a fixed-point number.

13.3   LOGICAL ARITHMETIC FUNCTIONS

The following functions operate on full machine words. The only acceptable
arguments are fixed-point numbers. These may be entered as octal or decimal
integers, or they may be the result of a previous computation.

$$\text{LOGOR } (x_1 \ x_2 \ \ldots \ x_n)$$

LOGOR is a special form of an indefinite number of arguments, the value of
which is the logical OR of all its arguments.

$$\text{LOGXOR } (x_1 \ x_2 \ \ldots \ x_n)$$

LOGXOR is a special form of an indefinite number of arguments, the value of
which is the logical exclusive OR of all its arguments.

$$\text{LOGAND } (x_1 \ x_2 \ \ldots \ x_n)$$

LOGAND is a special form of an indefinite number of arguments, the value of
which is the logical AND of all its arguments.

$$\text{LEFTSHIFT } (x \ n) = x * 2^n$$

LEFTSHIFT shifts its first argument left by the number of bits specified by
its second argument. If the second argument is negative, the first argument
will be shifted right.

Note:

> Various other numerical functions can be found on
> particular LISP systems. They are not standard, so
> they are not described here. Logarithmic and trigo-
> nometric functions are typical classes not covered
> here.

13.4 AN ARITHMETIC EXAMPLE

The power series expansion for SIN is given[8] by:

$$\text{SIN } x = x - \frac{x^3}{3!} + \frac{x^5}{5!} - \frac{x^7}{7!} + \frac{x^9}{9!} - \cdots$$

where x is in radians.

If $c_1 = 1$

$$c_3 = \frac{-1}{3!} = -1.666666667E\text{-}1$$

$$c_5 = \frac{1}{5!} = 8.333333333E\text{-}3$$

$$c_7 = \frac{-1}{7!} = -1.984126984E\text{-}4$$

$$c_9 = \frac{1}{9!} = 2.755731922E\text{-}6$$

we can approximate the power series as:

$$\text{SIN } x = c_1 x + c_3 x^3 + c_5 x^5 + c_7 x^7 + c_9 x^9$$

The LISP function SIN (x), where x is in radians, can now be defined in terms of this power series approximation.

```
    DEFINE ((
    (SIN (LAMBDA (X) (PLUS X (TIMES -1.666666667E-1 X X X)
                           (TIMES 8.333333333E-3 X X X X X)
                           (TIMES -1.984126984E-4 X X X X X X X)
                           (TIMES 2.755731922E-6 X X X X X X X X X)))) ))
```

If we factor out x^2 and write the power series in the form

$$\text{SIN } x = x(c_1 + x^2(c_3 + x^2(c_5 + x^2(c_7 + c_9 x^2))))$$

a more computationally efficient LISP program for SIN can be defined by using a nested lambda expression, as we need to compute x^2 only once.

```
DEFINE ((

(SIN (LAMBDA (X) ((LAMBDA (XSQ) (TIMES X (PLUS 1 (TIMES XSQ (PLUS -1.6666667E-1
    (TIMES XSQ (PLUS 8.333333333E-3 (TIMES XSQ (PLUS -1.984126984E-4
    (TIMES XSQ 2.755731922E-6)))))))))) (TIMES X X)))) ))
```

13.5   <u>EXERCISES</u>

Evaluate:

1. PLUS (1 2 3 4 5 6 7 8 9 10)
2. DIFFERENCE (99 3.14159)
3. TIMES (2 2 2 2 2 2 2 2 2 2)
4. ADD1 (77777Q)
5. SUB1 (1.0)
6. MINUS (-0)
7. MAX (10 12Q 10.000000001)
8. MIN (10 12Q 9.999999999)
9. QUOTIENT (55 3)
10. QUOTIENT (55.0 3Q)
11. REMAINDER (55 3)
12. REMAINDER (55 3.0)
13. DIVIDE (55 3)
14. DIVIDE (55 3.0)
15. DIVIDE (55 3Q)
16. ENTIER (123.4)
17. ENTIER (-123.4
18. ENTIER (0.7)
19. ENTIER (-0.7)
20. SQRT (25)
21. RECIP (3.0)
22. RECIP (3)
23. FLOAT (123456789)
24. ABSVAL (-3.14159)
25. LOGOR (77777Q 12345Q)
26. LOGOR (70707Q1 12345Q)
27. LOGXOR (77777Q1 12345Q)

28. LOGXOR (70707Q1 12345Q)

29. LOGAND (77777Q 12345Q)

30. LOGAND (70707Q1 12345Q)

31. LEFTSHIFT (7Q1 1)

32. LEFTSHIFT (7Q1 -1)

Define the following functions:

33. TRIPLE (X) = X + X + X

34. CUBE (X) = X^3

35. SIMPLEINTEREST (PRINCIPAL RATE YEARS) = P(1 + YR)

36. ANNUALCOMPOUND (P R Y) = $P(1 + R)^Y$

37. TIMECOMPOUND (P R Y T) = $P(1 + R/T)^{TY}$

38. The value of a two-by-two determinant is defined by:

$$\begin{vmatrix} a_{11} & a_{12} \\ a_{21} & a_{22} \end{vmatrix} = (a_{11}\,a_{22} - a_{12}\,a_{21})$$

Define the LISP function

$$\text{TWOBY } (a_{11}\ a_{12}\ a_{21}\ a_{22})$$

39. The value of a three-by-three determinant is defined by:

$$\begin{vmatrix} a_{11} & a_{12} & a_{13} \\ a_{21} & a_{22} & a_{23} \\ a_{31} & a_{32} & a_{33} \end{vmatrix} = a_{11} \begin{vmatrix} a_{22} & a_{23} \\ a_{32} & a_{33} \end{vmatrix} - a_{12} \begin{vmatrix} a_{21} & a_{23} \\ a_{31} & a_{33} \end{vmatrix} + a_{13} \begin{vmatrix} a_{21} & a_{22} \\ a_{31} & a_{32} \end{vmatrix}$$

Define the LISP function

$$\text{THREEBY } (a_{11}\ a_{12}\ \cdots\ a_{32}\ a_{33})$$

40. Given the three simultaneous equations

$$a_{11} u_1 + a_{12} u_2 + a_{13} u_3 = c_1$$

$$a_{21} u_1 + a_{22} u_2 + a_{23} u_3 = c_2$$

$$a_{31} u_1 + a_{32} u_2 + a_{33} u_3 = c_3$$

we can solve for any variable u_k by dividing two determinants. The denominator determinant, D, is as defined in problem 39. The numerator determinant is similar, but with the c_k terms replacing the coefficients of the u_k variables. For example:

$$u_2 = \frac{\begin{vmatrix} a_{11} & c_1 & a_{13} \\ a_{21} & c_2 & a_{23} \\ a_{31} & c_3 & a_{33} \end{vmatrix}}{D}$$

Define the LISP function

$$\text{SOLVE} (a_{11} \ a_{12} \ \cdots \ a_{32} \ a_{33} \ c_1 \ c_2 \ c_3)$$

which computes the value of all variables u_k for three simultaneous equations in three variables. (Hint: Use your definition of THREEBY and QUOTIENT.)

Try these equation sets:

1. $2u_1 + u_2 - 2u_3 = -6$

    $u_1 + u_2 + u_3 = 2$

    $-u_1 - 2u_2 + 3u_3 = 12$

2. $2u_1 + u_2 - 2u_3 = 5$

    $2u_1 + u_2 + 3u_3 = 6$

    $-u_1 - 2u_2 + 3u_3 = 12$

3. $15u_1 + 15u_2 + 15u_3 = 15$

$7u_1 + u_2 - 100u_3 = -100$

$-50u_1 + u_2 + u_3 = -16$

4. $u_1 + 2u_2 - 2u_3 = -12$

$u_1 + u_2 + u_3 = 6$

$-2u_1 - u_2 + 3u_3 = 2$

5. $-2u_1 + 2u_2 + u_3 = -24$

$u_1 + u_2 + u_3 = 29$

$3u_1 - u_2 - 2u_3 = 9$

CHAPTER 14.
RECURSIVE FUNCTIONS

The functions we have thus far defined have used lambda expressions, composition of forms, and conditional expressions. A still wider class of functions can be defined using these methods and the method of *recursion*.

It takes time and practice to think recursively, particularly if you have programming experience with the linear flow of control common with algebraic languages. You cannot be <u>taught</u> to think recursively, but you can <u>learn</u> to think recursively. To help you learn, I give some helpful heuristics, examples, and more examples.

Recursive functions may be defined in a manner similar to other functions using form composition. When we construct a form, such as

(CONS X Y)

we are making an explicit call upon the function CONS. CONS, in this case, is an already existing function. In a recursive function definition, for (say) function f, we likewise make explicit calls upon functions; however, one or more such calls are made upon the function f itself. The only apparent difference between calls upon CONS and calls upon f is that f is the function being described. But LISP doesn't mind. In most algebraic languages, the programmer is cautioned not to write subroutines that call upon themselves, since that is recursion and most algebraic languages cannot handle recursion. In LISP we do it all the time. For example, it is syntactically and semantically proper to write

    (<u>EXAMPLE</u> (LAMBDA (L) (COND ((NULL L) NIL)
                   (T (CONS (CAR L) (<u>EXAMPLE</u> (CDR L))))))))

We note that in this "do-nothing" function definition (i.e., EXAMPLE returns as its value a copy of the input list L), EXAMPLE makes an explicit call upon itself. EXAMPLE is thereby a recursive function.

Recursive definitions always define an idea in one or more special starting or finishing cases, and then define the idea in the general case in terms of a preceding or adjacent case. Let's see how this statement applies to a LISP problem.

14.1   A RECURSIVE EXAMPLE

Problem: given any list, such as

(A B C)

define the predicate

ATOMLIST (ℓ)

which is T if all elements of ℓ are atoms, and NIL otherwise. How shall we proceed? Essentially, we wish to perform the test

```
If ATOM A , then
     If ATOM B , then
          If ATOM C , then T;
          Else NIL
     Else NIL
Else NIL
```

which, as a LISP function, would be defined by

```
(ATOMLIST (LAMBDA (A B C)
     (COND ((ATOM A) (COND ((ATOM B) (ATOM C))
                                    (T F)))
          (T F))))
```

But this is __not__ a solution to our problem. We are not given A, B and C explicitly, but rather list ℓ, which can have any number of elements. We must do

(ATOM (CAR L))

to test an element of ℓ. Thus, we could write

```
(ATOMLIST (LAMBDA (L) (COND ((ATOM (CAR L))
        (COND ((ATOM (CADR L)) (ATOM (CADDR L)))
        (T F))) (T F))))
```

But this last definition solves the problem when we know list ℓ has exactly
three elements. How about the general case where we do not know the length
of list ℓ, or even when we do know, but where ℓ is very long? We don't want
to write

```
(CADDDDDDDDDDDDDDDDDDDDR L)
```

even if we could, for a 20-element list.

The proper strategy is to test the first element of the list with the expression

```
(ATOM (CAR L))
```

If it is NIL, we exit NIL. If it is T, we need to test the second list element.
If it proves T, then we test the third element, etc. But note, if after we
test the first element, we remove the first element from the list, then the
second element becomes the first element of the new list and we can apply the
same test to the new list. The new list is

```
(CDR L)
```

and the test is applied recursively. Thus, we can write

```
(ATOMLIST (LAMBDA (L)
        (COND ((ATOM (CAR L)) (ATOMLIST (CDR L))) (T F))))
```

which is recursive. What we have done is to first examine the (CAR L). If it
is an atom, we reduce the list ℓ by taking the (CDR L) to get a new list. Then
we test this new list with ATOMLIST. If we ever find a non-atomic element, the
conditional will return NIL.

This last definition almost works, but not quite. It fails because we haven't
set up a terminal condition. As it stands now, unless we exit NIL because some
element of the list was non-atomic, we will recur again and again, reducing ℓ
each time until ℓ no longer has elements but is NIL. And then we would try

recurring once more and try to take the CDR of NIL. There's the rub: (CDR NIL)
is undefined. To exit properly, we must test for the terminal condition. In
this case

(NULL L)

will suffice. Thus our final, _correct_ recursive definition for ATOMLIST is:

```
DEFINE ((
(ATOMLIST (LAMBDA (L) (COND ((NULL L) T )
   ((ATOM (CAR L)) (ATOMLIST (CDR L)))
   (T F)))) ))
```

Note that if we ever encounter the null condition, ATOMLIST is T since all prior
elements must have tested true. We perform the null test first to allow ℓ to
be completely general, including the empty list, NIL. Note then that

ATOMLIST (NIL) = T

14.2   SOME HELPFUL HEURISTICS

The following heuristics can be used as aids in defining recursive functions:

1. Start with a trivial case, or a terminal case in which the rule for
    computation is known. Some typical trivial or terminal cases are:

    for S-expressions, atoms;
    for lists, NIL;
    for numbers, 0,1.

2. For the non-trivial, non-terminal case, try to reduce the expression
    to a case "nearer" the trivial case.

3. Combine the trivial or terminal case with the other, using the trivial
    or terminal case first in a conditional expression.

4. Always check your definition by trying several simple--but not all
    trivial--examples.

Let's try these heuristics on the recursive definition of FACTORIAL, where

$$n! = \text{UNDEFINED, for } n < 0$$
$$= 1, \text{ for } n = 0$$
$$= n * (n-1)!, \text{ for } n > 0$$

1. The argument of FACTORIAL is a number. Therefore, the trivial case is for n = 0.

2. In the trivial case where n = 0, then

    FACTORIAL (N) = (COND ((ZEROP N) 1))

3. If n is not zero, then we can break n! into the product of two parts, n and (n-1)!, since (n-1)! moves us nearer the trivial case (2). Thus,

    FACTORIAL (N) = (TIMES N (FACTORIAL (SUB1 N)))

4. Now, combining the two cases (2) and (3) conditionally with the trivial case first, we get

    DEFINE ((
    (FACTORIAL (LAMBDA (N) (COND ((ZEROP N) 1)
                                (T (TIMES N (FACTORIAL (SUB1 N))))))))))

Let's trace through this example for n = 3.

         Arguments of FACTORIAL = 3, descend (recursion)
            Arguments of FACTORIAL = 2, descend (recursion)
               Arguments of FACTORIAL = 1, descend (recursion)
                  Arguments of FACTORIAL = 0, terminal condition
                  Value of FACTORIAL = 1, ascend
               Value of FACTORIAL = 1, ascend
            Value of FACTORIAL = 2, ascend
         Value of FACTORIAL = 6, complete

What we have effectively done in this example is to create

    FACTORIAL (3) = (TIMES 3 (TIMES 2 (TIMES 1 1)))

In general, we will descend as deep as is necessary to reach the terminal case and the effective computation will be

$$\text{FACTORIAL (n)} = (\text{TIMES n (TIMES n--1} \dots (\text{TIMES 2 (TIMES 1 1))} \dots))$$

14.3   MORE RECURSIVE EXAMPLES

The following function definitions are pedagogical devices. Although these functions are available in LISP, these definitions may not exactly replicate those in a given system.

1.   The function EQUAL (x y) that we saw in Chapter 12 can be defined by:

```
DEFINE (( (EQUAL (LAMBDA (X Y)
            (COND ((ATOM X) (EQ X Y))
                  ((ATOM Y) NIL)
                  ((EQUAL (CAR X) (CAR Y)) (EQUAL (CDR X) (CDR Y)))
                  (T NIL)))) ))
```

This definition uses EQ and hence does not handle numbers.

2.   The function APPEND has two arguments, both lists. The value is a list formed by appending the second list to the first. For example:

```
APPEND ((A B) (D E F)) = (A B D E F)

DEFINE (( (APPEND (LAMBDA (X Y)
            (COND ((NULL X) Y)
                  (T (CONS (CAR X) (APPEND (CDR X) Y)))))) ))
```

3.   The function LAST has one argument, a list. The value is the last top-level element of the list.

```
DEFINE (( (LAST (LAMBDA (L)
            (COND ((NULL L) NIL)
                  ((NULL (CDR L)) (CAR L))
                  (T (LAST (CDR L))))) ))
```

4. Given a list of pairs of the format

$$((a_1\ b_1)\ (a_2\ b_2)\ \ldots\ (a_n\ b_n))$$

the function ASSOC (E L) searches the list L for a pair, the first element of which is equal to E. If such a pair is found, it is returned as the value of ASSOC. Otherwise, the value is NIL, e.g.,

ASSOC (AA ((A B) (C D) (AA FOO))) = (AA FOO)

DEFINE (((ASSOC (LAMBDA (E L)
             (COND ((NULL L) NIL)
                   ((EQUAL E (CAAR L)) (CAR L))
                   (T (ASSOC E (CDR L))))))))

5. The predicate MEMBER described in Chapter 12 can be defined by:

DEFINE (((MEMBER (LAMBDA (A X)
             (COND ((ATOM X) (EQUAL A X))
                   ((EQUAL A (CAR X)) T)
                   (T (MEMBER A (CDR X)))))))

This definition uses EQUAL, and thus allows the value of A to be any S-expression.

14.4   LABEL NOTATION

Earlier we saw that we could compose and evaluate top-level lambda expressions. These were _temporary_ lambda expressions. If we named them, we could with DEFINE make them _permanent_ functions. Recursive expressions point up an inadequacy in lambda notation that requires us to define as permanent, recursive functions that we wish to use as temporary functions. This difficulty stems from the inability to call the function from within itself, since the lambda expression is not named. (When a function is recursive, it must be given a name.) To resolve this difficulty and thereby allow composition and evaluation of temporary recursive functions, we use the special form LABEL.

To write temporary functions that can call themselves recursively, we write

                    (LABEL name lambda-expression)

where "name" is any literal atom you choose as the name for the given lambda
expression.

Example:

                    (LABEL DUMMY (LAMBDA (X)
                        (COND ((ATOM X) X)
                            (T (DUMMY (CAR X)))))) (argument list)

Label notation, as this is called, creates temporary expressions that, like the
temporary lambda expressions seen earlier, may be evaluated at the top level.
Also, like temporary lambda expressions, the expression must be entered again
each time it is applied to a different argument list. In fact, that is the
meaning of "temporary expression" as used here. Of course, we can always use
DEFINE to create permanent functions rather than repeatedly using LAMBDA or
LABEL. In practice, temporary lambda expressions are used frequently, but LABEL
is seldom used, the preference being to attach the name by use of DEFINE.

14.5   EXERCISES

    1. Evaluate

            (LABEL NAME (LAMBDA (X) (COND ((ATOM X) X) (T (NAME (CDR X))))))

        for the following arguments:

            A
            (A . B)
            ((X . Y) . (X . Z))
            (A B C)
            (A (C . E))

    2. Evaluate

            (LABEL MATCH (LAMBDA (X Y)
                (COND ((OR (NULL X) (NULL Y)) (QUOTE NO))
                    ((EQ (CAR X) (CAR Y)) (CAR X))
                    (T (MATCH (CDR X) (CDR Y))))))
                            -99-

for the following arguments:

```
(X) (X)
(A B E) (J O E)
(K A Y) (E V E)
( E L L I N) (H E L E N)
```

3. Define

```
(TWIST (LAMBDA (S)
   (COND ((ATOM S) S)
           (T (CONS (TWIST (CDR S))
                     (TWIST (CAR S)))))))
```

Evaluate

```
TWIST (A)
TWIST ((A . B))
TWIST (((A . B) . C))
TWIST ((A B C))
TWIST (((A . B)))
```

4. Let us plan how to define, recursively, the function

SUM $(x\ y) = x + y$

using only the functions ADD1 and SUB1, and the predicate ZEROP.

The trivial case is $y = 0$. Then the value of SUM would be the value of x.

We can reduce the general case, $y \neq 0$, to the trivial one by reducing y by 1, increasing x by 1, and recurring on these values. This gives rise to the following definition:

```
(SUM (LAMBDA (X Y)
   (COND ((ZEROP Y) X)
           (T (SUM (ADD1 X) (SUB1 Y))))))
```

Using this definition, show the arguments and values of SUM each time it is entered for

SUM (1 2)

5. Define recursively, using only the functions ADD1, SUB1, and ZEROP

PROD (x y) = x * y

Hint:

If y = 0, then the product is trivially zero. If not, then the product is the SUM of x and the PROD of x and y-1.

6. We know that division is essentially repeated subtraction, and that the remainder in division is the residue when subtraction is no longer possible. Therefore, define recursively

REMXY (x y)

which yields the remainder resulting from the division of x by y.

7. Define the recursive function COUNT having one argument. The argument may be any S-expression. The value of COUNT is the number of atoms in the argument.

8. The Fibonacci series is a sequence of integers. The first two terms are 1 and 1, respectively. After that, each term of the series is the sum of the preceding two terms.

The Fibonacci series begins as

1, 1, 2, 3, 5, 8, 13, 21, ...

Define the function FIBB(N) that returns as its value the Nth term of the series.

9. The greatest common divisor (G.C.D.) of two whole numbers is the largest number that will exactly divide both of them. Euclid gave an algorithm, which can be stated in English.

> The G.C.D. of x and y is:
> If x is greater than y, then find the G.C.D. of y and x. Else, if the remainder of y divided by x is zero, then the value is x. Else, the value is the G.C.D. of x and the remainder of y divided by x.

Use this algorithm to define GCD (x y); e.g.,

$$GCD \ (7 \ 7) = 7$$
$$GCD \ (19 \ 7) = 1$$
$$GCD \ (28 \ 35) = 7$$

10. Define

$$AMONG \ (a \ \ell)$$

which is a predicate that is T if and only if the atom a is among the top-level elements of list ℓ.

$$AMONG \ (X \ (A \ B \ X)) = T$$
$$AMONG \ (X \ (A \ B \ (X))) = NIL$$

11. Define

$$INSIDE \ (a \ e)$$

which is a predicate that is T if and only if the atom a appears anywhere at any level in the S-expression e.

$$INSIDE \ (X \ (A \ B \ X)) = T$$
$$INSIDE \ (X \ (A \ (X) \ B)) = T$$
$$INSIDE \ (X \ (A \ . \ (B \ . \ X))) = T$$

12. Define

COPYN (x n)

which will put n copies of x on a list; e.g.,

COPYN ((A B) 3) = ((A B) (A B) (A B))

Most LISP systems have functions LENGTH, UNION, INTERSECTION, REVERSE, and
SUBST available as built-in functions. If you err in redefining such functions
to the computer, you can "crash" the system. For that reason, I have avoided
name clashes in the following problems, but realize the direct correspondence
between these names and LENGTHS, UNIONS, INTERSECT, REVERSAL, and REPLACE,
respectively.

13. Define

LENGTHS (ℓ)

which counts the number of top-level elements of a list, e.g.,

LENGTHS ((A B (C D) E)) = 4

14. Define

UNIONS (x y)

which returns a list that contains every element that is in one list
or the other or both. The order in which the elements are presented
is first, all the elements that are in the first list, x, and not in
the second list, y, and second, all elements in the second list, y,
whether or not they are in list x.

Hint:

Use the function MEMBER.

UNIONS ((U V W) (W X Y)) = (U V W X Y)
UNIONS ((A B C) (B C D)) = (A B C D)

15. Define

        INTERSECT (x y)

which returns a list of elements common to both list x and list y.

        INTERSECT ((A B C) (B C D)) = (B C)
        INTERSECT ((A B C) (D E F)) = NIL

16. Define

        REVERSAL (ℓ)

which reverses the order of top-level elements of the list ℓ; e.g.,

        REVERSAL (((A B) D (D E) G)) = (G (D E) D (A B))

Hint:

    Use APPEND as given in the earlier examples.

17. Define

        PAIRS (ℓ1 ℓ2)

which produces a list of dotted pairs of the elements of two lists
of equal length; e.g.,

        PAIRS ((ONE TWO THREE) (1 2 3)) = ((ONE . 1) (TWO . 2) (THREE . 3))

18. Define

        DELETE (a ℓ)

which produces a new list in which all references to the atom a have
been deleted from the top level of list ℓ; e.g.,

        DELETE (Y (X Y Z)) = (X Z)

19. Define the predicate

        INSEQ (ℓ)

which is T if list ℓ contains a numerical sequence in proper ascending or descending order, and NIL otherwise.

Hint:

      Use an auxiliary function INSEQA that tests ascending order only. Use INSEQA with REVERSE (a system function analogous to REVERSAL above) to test descending order.

          INSEQ (1 2 3 4) = T
          INSEQ (40 30 2 1) = T
          INSEQ (1 23 24 27 26 30) = NIL
          INSEQ (10.0 9 8 7.4 2.3) = T
          INSEQ (A B C D E) = NIL

20. Define

          REPLACE (a b x)

which is a function that replaces the atom b by the atom a for every occurrence of b in x. a, b, and x are S-expressions.

          REPLACE (A B (A B C D)) = (A A C D)
          REPLACE (TWO TO (WE TO HAVE TO CATS)) = (WE TWO HAVE TWO CATS)

CHAPTER 15.
THE PROGRAM FEATURE

The LISP 1.5 *program feature*, which is called by the special form PROG, allows us to write an ALGOL-like program containing statements to be executed. It provides the capability to perform iteration by allowing looping and the use of temporary variables.

15.1   PROG FORMAT

As you recall, a lambda expression has the following syntax:

(LAMBDA *varlist body*)

The PROG form becomes the *body* or part of the *body* of a lambda expression. Like all forms, it is an S-expression; it has the structure

(PROG *varlist statements*)

The list of variables, *varlist*, as with lambda expressions, contains the variables of the PROG required by the *statements*. The *statements* are themselves S-expressions.

Thus, the complete lambda expression with the PROG form has the structure

(LAMBDA (*lambda-variables*) (PROG (*program-variables*) *statements*))

15.2   PROGRAM VARIABLES

We usually call the variables associated with the lambda expression *lambda variables*, and those associated with the PROG, *program* or *prog variables*. The list of program variables, just like the list of lambda variables, must always be present in the structure of the expression. If we have none, then the list is entered as NIL or ( ).

As with lambda variables, program variables are also *dummy variables*; we usually think of dummy variables as being either lambda or program variables.

Unlike lambda variables, which have no value until lambda conversion, program variables always have value NIL until they are changed or set by statements within the PROG.

Two functions are used to set dummy variables (i.e., lambda or program variables), SET and SETQ.

SET is a function of two variables, and has the form:

$$(SET\ v_1\ v_2)$$

which can be read as "set the value of v_1 equal to the value of v_2". Both variables v_1 and v_2 can be (and usually are) S-expressions themselves. They are evaluated and the value of v_1 must be a literal atom. The value of v_2 is bound to the value of v_1. If we wish to set a specific program variable, we must always use QUOTE, e.g.,

$$(SET\ (QUOTE\ PI)\ 3.14159)$$

SETQ is like SET, but for convenience, SETQ always _quotes_ its first argument. The "Q" in the name "SETQ" is to remind us of this fact, e.g.,

$$(SETQ\ PI\ 3.14159)$$

SET and SETQ return as their values the value of the second argument, v_2.

15.3   FLOW OF CONTROL

Within the PROG form, the flow of control is like that of FORTRAN or ALGOL. Each program statement is a form, and the sequence of statements is a sequence of forms. The simplest S-expressions are literal atoms, and these are used as _statement labels_ or names for the statements that follow. For example,

```
          (SETQ PI 3.14159)
     LOC1 (SETQ R N)
          (SETQ AREA (TIMES R PI R))
```

has atomic symbol LOC1 as a name for the statement

```
          (SETQ R N)
```

Statements are normally executed in sequence. Executing a statement means evaluating the form. Program statements are often executed for their effect rather than for their value, as with SETQ above. The GO statement is a perfect example of execution for effect rather than value. GO is a function used to cause a transfer to a named statement. It is a function of one argument that is not evaluated--that argument being a statement label, e.g.,

(GO LOC1)

To exit from a PROG, we use RETURN. RETURN is a function of one argument, and the argument is evaluated. The value of the argument is returned as the value of the PROG. A RETURN statement terminates the PROG form and no further statements are executed.

We can also exit from a PROG without the RETURN statement by just "running out" of statements. In that case, the value of the PROG is always NIL.

PROG statements can be constructed from any of the expressions available in LISP. They may be conditional or recursive expressions. They may even be lambda or program expressions, thereby allowing nesting of program expressions.

15.4   SOME CAUTIONS

Conditional expressions as program statements have a useful peculiarity. If there are only NIL clauses, instead of an error indication (which would otherwise occur on some systems), the program continues with the next statement. In other words, the program "falls through" the conditional expression if there are no true conditions. This peculiarity is true only for conditional expressions that are statements of a PROG. Nested conditional forms used in the PROG expression behave in the normal manner (see Chapter 11).

For some LISP systems, GO may be used only as a statement of a PROG or immediately inside a COND that is a statement of a PROG. Most implementations have removed this restriction.

If we nest a PROG within a PROG, within a PROG, etc., the GO, RETURN, SETQ, etc., will have a *scope* local to the most recent PROG. For example, GO cannot transfer to a statement label within another higher- or lower-level PROG.

Similarly, RETURN takes you "up" one level to the next higher expression. In certain special cases, SETQ may be used on variables defined by a higher-level PROG. These variables are then called *free variables* and require special attention. We will discuss variables and their bindings in the next chapter.

15.5 EXAMPLES

In the last chapter we saw the recursive definition of FACTORIAL. Let's contrast that expression with one using the program feature.

FACTORIAL--recursive definition

```
DEFINE ((
(FACTORIAL (LAMBDA (N)
(COND ((ZEROP N) 1) (T (TIMES N (FACTORIAL (SUB1 N)))))))
))
```

FACTORIAL--program feature

```
DEFINE ((
(FACTORIAL (LAMBDA (N) (PROG (Y)
                       (SETQ Y 1)
             TAG1    (COND ((ZEROP N) (RETURN Y)))
                       (SETQ Y (TIMES N Y))
                       (SETQ N (SUB1 N))
                       (GO TAG1))))

))
```

In these examples, the recursive definition appears to be simpler than the one using the program feature. In other problems it may be otherwise. The choice of whether to use the program feature or to use "pure LISP" in writing a program, depends in large measure on the problem. Style in programming is often, however, the stronger influence--as noted by Fisher Black.[9]

15.6 PROG2

The function PROG2 is distantly related to PROG. It is a function of two arguments that evaluates both its arguments in order, i.e., argument one first, argument two second. PROG2 has as its value the value of its second argument.

Thus,

$$(LAMBDA (X Y) (PROG2 (CONS X Y) Y)) (A B) = B$$

The utility of PROG2 can be seen in the following example.

Example:

Given a list of numbers, define the function SORT,
which sorts these numbers into odd or even and
returns a list of two sublists of the form:

((odd-count list-of-odd-numbers) (even-count list-of-even-numbers))

```
SORT ((1 2 3 4 5)) = ((3 (5 3 1)) (2 (4 2)))
SORT (( 1 3 5 7 9)) = ((5 (9 7 5 3 1)) (0 NIL))
SORT ((2 4 6 8 10)) = ((0 NIL) (5 (10 8 6 4 2)))

DEFINE ((
(SORT (LAMBDA (X) (PROG (ODD EVEN ODDCNT EVENCNT L)
        (SETQ L X) (SETQ ODDCNT 0) (SETQ EVENCNT 0)
LOOP    (COND ((NULL L) (RETURN (LIST (LIST ODDCNT ODD)
                                (LIST EVENCNT EVEN))))
              ((EVENP (CAR L))
               (SETQ EVEN (PROG2 (SETQ EVENCNT (ADD1 EVENCNT))
                                 (CONS (CAR L) EVEN))))
              (T (SETQ ODD (PROG2 (SETQ ODDCNT (ADD1 ODDCNT))
                                  (CONS (CAR L) ODD)))))
        (SETQ L (CDR L))
        (GO LOOP) ))) ))
```

Note:

The conditional clause

```
(T (SETQ ODD (PROG2 (SETQ ODDCNT (ADD1 ODDCNT))
                    (CONS (CAR L) ODD))))
```

could have been written

```
(T (PROG2 (SETQ ODDCNT (ADD1 ODDCNT))
          (SETQ ODD (CONS (CAR L) ODD)))))
```

I chose the former method to emphasize the return of the value of the last argument. In fact, some systems generalize PROG2 to PROGN, a special form of an indefinite number of arguments that returns the value of the last argument. PROGN can be defined as a macro (see Chapter 19) in terms of PROG2.

15.7   EXERCISES

1. Using PROG, define the function

        NEGCNT (ℓ)

    which counts the number of negative numbers at the top level of list ℓ.

2. The discriminant b^2-4ac, of a second degree equation of the form

        $$ax^2 + bxy + cy^2 + dx + ey + f = 0$$

    can be used to determine the type of curve represented by the equation, according to the following schedule:

    1. A parabola if discriminant = 0
    2. An ellipse if discriminant < 0
    3. A hyperbola if discriminant > 0

    Define

        CURVE (a b c)

    which evaluates to PARABOLA, ELLIPSE, or HYPERBOLA as a function of the numerical values of arguments a, b, and c.

3. The recursive definition for LENGTHS is:

        DEFINE ((
        (LENGTHS (LAMBDA (M)
            (COND ((NULL M) 0)
                (T (ADD1 (LENGTHS (CDR M)))))))))

    Define LENGTHS using PROG.

4. The recursive definition for LAST is:

```
          DEFINE ((
          (LAST (LAMBDA (L)
              (COND ((NULL L) NIL)
                    ((NULL (CDR L)) (CAR L))
                    (T (LAST (CDR L)))))) ))
```

Define LAST using PROG.

Define the following functions using PROG. (See Chapter 14, problems 16, 17, and 18.)

5. REVERSAL
6. PAIRS
7. DELETE

8. Each different arrangement of all or a part of a set of things is called a "permutation". The number of permutations of n different things taken r at a time is

$$P(n,r) = n! \ / \ (n-r)!$$

Define, with and without PROG (using FACTORIAL),

$$PERMUT \ (n \ r) = n! \ / \ (n-r)!$$

9. Each of the groups or relations which can be made by taking part or all of a set of things, without regard to the arrangement of the things in a group, is called a "combination". The number of combinations of n different things taken r at a time is

$$C(n,r) = n! \ / \ r! \ (n-r)!$$

Define, with and without PROG

$$COMBIN \ (n \ r) = n! \ / \ r! \ (n-r)!$$

10. An interesting way to obtain the combinations of n different things taken r at a time is to construct Pascal's triangle. The triangle looks like this:

```
                              ↙ r=0
n=0 →                1    ↙ r=1
n=1 →              1   1      ↙ r=2
n=2 →            1   2   1  ↙ r=3
n=3 →          1   3   3   1   ↙ r=4
n=4 →        1   4   6   4   1   ↙ r=5
n=5 →      1   5   10  10  5   1
```

Given the pseudo-function PRINT, which takes one S-expression as its argument and prints the value of that argument, e.g.,

.... (PRINT (LIST (QUOTE A) (QUOTE B) 3 (QUOTE C))) = (A B 3 C)

and ignoring the triangular format, use your definition for COMBIN to define

PASCAL (n)

which prints Pascal's triangle to depth n, e.g.,

PASCAL (5) =

(1)
(1 1)
(1 2 1)
(1 3 3 1)
(1 4 6 4 1)
(1 5 10 10 5 1)
NIL

CHAPTER 16.

VARIABLES AND THEIR BINDING

So far, for the sake of convenience, I have been intentionally vague in describing the mechanisms used by LISP to bind variables. This chapter attempts to clarify what we have been doing in this regard.

A variable is a symbol that is used to represent an argument of a function. Thus, one might write a + b, where a = 341 and b = 216. In this situation, no confusion can result, and all will agree that the answer is 557. In order to arrive at this result, it is necessary to substitute the actual numbers for the variables, and then add the two numbers (on an adding machine, for instance).

One reason why there is no ambiguity in this case is that "a" and "b" are not acceptable inputs for an adding machine, and it is therefore obvious that they merely represent the actual arguments. In LISP, the situation can be much more complicated. An atomic symbol may be either a variable or a constant. To further complicate the situation, an argument may be an arbitrary symbolic constant that superficially looks like an expression to be evaluated. The intuitive approach is no longer adequate. In the examples so far, we have seen functions applied to specific arguments to get specific results. We have also provided for arbitrary arguments by means of *bound variables* in LAMBDA and PROG expressions.

16.1   BOUND VARIABLES

Rule:

An atom is always evaluated. If you wish to suppress evaluation, quote it. Some atoms, such as T, NIL, and numbers in particular, are permanent constants.

The implication of this rule is that all non-quoted atoms are bound variables. But what does this mean? It means that all non-quoted literal atoms are considered to be variables that have values, and we say that a value is "bound to the variable". This value can be any S-expression. The binding is in actuality an association of data internal to the LISP system that is recognized and manipulated by the LISP system when an expression is evaluated. To understand bound variables adequately, we must examine more closely how these associations are constructed internal to LISP. The methods for binding depend upon the nature of the LISP system. Interpreters bind variables differently than do compilers. Lambda and program variables are examples of bound variables. In the expression

$$(\text{LAMBDA } (A \ B \ C) \ (\text{PROG } (X \ Y \ Z) \ \ldots \ ))$$

the lambda variables A, B, C, and the program variables, X, Y, Z are all bound variables.

16.2   THE A-LIST

In some interpretive LISP systems, whenever a lambda or program expression is encountered, the variables to be bound are placed on the *association list* or *a-list*. The a-list is a list of dotted pairs of the form

$$((u_1 \cdot v_1) \ (u_2 \cdot v_2) \ \ldots \ (u_n \ v_n))$$

where u_i is the name of a variable and v_i is its value, or binding.

Lambda or program variables are paired with their values and the pairs are appended to the **front** (leftmost) end of the existing a-list, with older bindings further back. When we exit from a function, the bindings for that expression are removed, and the a-list is shortened. The bindings for a particular expression are its *context*.

During form evaluation, all references to dummy variables are references to the a-list. The a-list is searched, front to back, for the first occurrence of the variable. (The function ASSOC is useful for this purpose.) The CDR of the pair is then the value of the variable. If a function is recursive, there will be multiple occurrences of its variables on the a-list, each representing the context of the function at some prior call. During evaluation, only the first occurrence of the variable is used, corresponding to the current context of the function.

16.3   FREE VARIABLES

An expression to be evaluated has a context given by the current bindings of all its variables. Since the value of the expression depends upon the current bindings, the value of the expression depends upon its context. Change the context and you (probably) change the value of the expression.

On the other hand, variables are defined by expressions; their *scope* of definition, in which a given binding may be retrieved, is restricted to the expression in which they were defined. Outside that scope, the binding, or even the variable itself, does not exist. For lambda variables, the scope is the *body* of the lambda expression. For program variables, the scope is the *statements* of the program expression.

Frequently, however, an expression may reference a variable it has not defined. If this reference is to be meaningful, the variable must be defined and bound at some higher level such that its scope encompasses the immediate expression. We speak of such references as "free references" and call the variables *free variables*.

Examine the expression

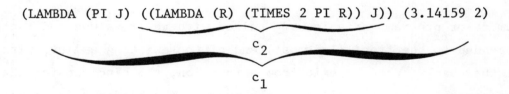

$$\text{(LAMBDA (PI J) ((LAMBDA (R) (TIMES 2 PI R)) J)) (3.14159 2)}$$

PI is a free variable in the innermost lambda expression, c_2.

After bindings have been established by lambda conversion, the a-list looks as follows during the evaluation of the innermost lambda expression.

$$\text{((R . 2) (PI . 3.14159) (J . 2) ...)}$$

The contexts for expressions c_1 and c_2 are noted.

When the form

$$(TIMES\ 2\ PI\ R)$$

is evaluated, the a-list is searched for the values of variables R and PI. R
is found in the current context, labeled c_2, but PI is found at a higher context
level, labeled c_1. Thus, free variables are evaluated by searching through the
complete a-list, independent of context, until the first occurrence of the
variable is encountered. If a free variable has not been bound at some higher
level, no association will be found on the a-list and an error will result.

16.4   CONSTANTS

Quoting data is one way to realize constants in a form. Using free variables is
another method. But what if we wish to use names for constant data, for clarity
in programming or for the simple, practical reason that the name may be shorter
than the data and hence easier to write? When a variable always has a certain
value, irrespective of the current a-list, we call it a *constant*. This is
accomplished by means of *value cells* also called *special cells*.

Every literal atom has a value cell that may contain the binding to a constant.
For conventional LISP interpretive systems, the value cell is on the atom's
property list (see Chapter 19) under the indicator APVAL (for "apply value").
For compiler-based systems, and some more recent interpretive systems, the value
cell is part of the atomic structure of a literal atom (see Chapter 19).

When a constant is used, it is used as a free variable and the binding is
retrieved from the value cell, not the a-list. The internal mechanism which
tells LISP when to examine the value cell and when to search the a-list is
extremely implementation-dependent and beyond the scope of this text. In fact,
on recent systems there is no a-list at all, but some other more efficient
storage mechanism. Our primary concern here is to learn how to establish
bindings in the value cell.

Lambda conversion establishes bindings on the a-list (or equivalent repository
with more recent systems), not in the value cell. Value cell bindings are
often called "zero-level" bindings since they are established at the top-most

level of LISP. They are also called "global" bindings since the scope of the bindings encompasses all levels of expressions. Zero-level bindings can be established on most systems with the pseudo-functions CSET and CSETQ.

CSET acts like a function of two variables of the form

$$(CSET\ v_1\ v_2)$$

Both v_1 and v_2 are evaluated; v_1 must evaluate to a literal atom. The value of v_2 is placed in the value cell of the literal atom value of v_1. For example,

$$(CSET\ (QUOTE\ PI)\ 3.14159)$$

will bind the number 3.14159 to the atom PI.

CSETQ is like CSET except that it quotes its first argument, e.g.,

$$(CSETQ\ PI\ 3.14159)$$

Both CSET and CSETQ return the value of v_2.

Note that CSET at the top level is

$$CSET\ (PI\ 3.14159)$$

since EVALQUOTE quotes its arguments. We cannot use CSETQ at the top level because a double quote would occur (once by EVALQUOTE, once by CSETQ itself) for v_1 and it would not then evaluate to the manditory literal atom.

16.5   COMPILER BINDINGS

The binding of variables on an a-list is adequate for interpreters where the lambda expression is saved and evaluated each time; but it is inadequate for compiled functions since the symbolic expressions are translated into machine code and discarded. Compiled functions also run one or two orders of magnitude faster than interpreted functions by eliminating the costly a-list searches during evaluation.

There are two types of variables in compiled functions: *special variables* and *ordinary variables*.

Accordingly, variables may be bound in one of two places, in the value cell, or on an internal last-in-first-out (LIFO) stack or table referred to as the *push-down list*.

If a variable is an ordinary one, a storage location is reserved for it on the push-down list when the expression in which it is defined is evaluated. Other functions cannot find this private cell, making it impossible to use it as a free variable on most systems. Ordinary variables are lambda and program variables, i.e., dummy variables. After the parent expression is evaluated and evaluation moves to a higher-level expression, the reserved location is released, and its contents are lost, analogous to releasing context on an a-list.

Special variables are used for constants and free variables. Such variables have indicators associated with their names (in some implementation-dependent manner) designating them as special variables. When a function uses a variable freely, the quantity in the value cell is the value of the variable.

Free variables must be bound in the value cell if the proper binding is to be retrieved during evaluation. To convey this information to the LISP compiler, you must declare free variables as special cases before compilation. In most systems, declarations are made with the pseudo-function SPECIAL.

SPECIAL is a pseudo-function of <u>one</u> argument, a <u>list</u> of all the variables used free in the functions being defined. Thus,

SPECIAL ((PI DOG))

declares the atoms PI and DOG as special cases; any time PI or DOG is used as a free variable, values will be bound and retrieved from that atom's value cell. You may "un-special" any special variable with the function UNSPECIAL. UNSPECIAL is the inverse of, but in the same form as, SPECIAL. Thus,

UNSPECIAL ((PI DOG))

removes the special status from the atoms PI and DOG.

16.6   <u>EXERCISES</u>

This chapter has no exercises because of the different treatment given variables by different implementations. The areas of common treatment, such as dummy variables, have been covered by previous chapters. For more information and exercises, consult the LISP expert for your system.

CHAPTER 17.
DEBUGGING, INPUT-OUTPUT, AND SUPERVISORS

LISP, like many current programming languages, suffers from a lack of standardization in the areas of debugging and input-output. I don't wish to imply that LISP is weak in these areas. On the contrary, LISP systems have extremely powerful debugging aids. This chapter presents the more common features available on most systems, though even here minor differences in definitions appear across various implementations. In addition, more recent systems have capitalized on new technological advances (such as time-sharing and interactive on-line operation), and have extended these features in interesting and exciting ways, so that the reader is encouraged to explore these areas with his own system.

17.1   PROGRAM DEBUGGING

Errors that fault a LISP program generally fall into two broad categories: syntax errors, and semantic errors. Often, the symptoms of failure fall in one category, whereas the cause of failure stems from errors in the other category. A perfect example is the poorly formed conditional expression, which--even though parentheses may balance out--is incorrectly structured.

Elaine Gord[10] has noted some problem areas in LISP debugging based on her experience. From this experience--and from my own--I have compiled the following checklists of high-probability error sources in LISP.

Syntactic Error Sources

1. READ balks because of an insufficient number of right parentheses.

2. READ balks because an S-expression begins with a right parenthesis--a symptom of an excess of right parentheses in the prior S-expression read.

3. READ balks because an S-expression written in dot-notation has "too many dots"--a symptom of a poorly formed S-expression.

4. READ balks because of an illegally spelled atom. Check the legal syntax of numbers and literal atoms allowed by your system. Watch out for the classic error of interchanging the numbers zero and one, and the letters "O" and "I". Also, if the S-expression being read was originally produced by a LISP printout on card, tape, or disc, any unusually spelled literal atoms previously entered as strings (see Paragraph 17.6) have probably been stripped of the string quoting apparatus and printed as a literal string. You cannot re-read such strings without restoring the string quoting apparatus.

5. A run-time error occurs due to poorly structured forms. Check your parentheses according to the legal syntax for LAMBDA and PROG expressions, for COND and SELECT, for DEFINE, and other special forms.

6. A run-time error occurs due to poorly delimited atoms. The characters blank, comma, left and right parenthesis always terminate the name of an atom (other terminators may also exit on given systems). Check that all atoms have been properly delimited. Particularly, check the local system conventions for atom composition across card (or line) boundaries.

Semantic Error Sources

1. Check syntax error possibilities.

2. Undefined functions may not have been defined through over-sight. Otherwise, check _your_ spelling and the proper _system_ spelling for the function you want.

3. Watch out for duplicate names. You may have duplicate names for dummy variables (if they are in different LAMBDA or PROG forms), but not for CSET variables or functions. Beware particularly of names used internally by the system. Check with your local LISP expert for all system names (both

variables and functions) that may clash with user names.

4. Lambda conversion errors result when an improper number of arguments are supplied to the function. Furthermore, the order of the arguments may be in error.

5. Wrong arguments cause errors. Check that the arguments are of the proper type and form. If the function expects numbers, don't give it lists. Also, functions that use CAAR, CADR, etc., presuppose a list containing lists as elements.

6. Familiarize yourself with the differences between CONS, LIST, APPEND, and other list-making functions. You may have selected the wrong function and not produced the desired value.

7. Watch your predicates in conditional expressions. Are they the negation of what you really want? Is the conditional expression checking for all cases, and in the proper order?

8. Terminating conditions of recursive functions are very important. Check that you have the right conditions, the proper number of them, and have situated them in the proper place in the recursive function definition.

17.2 DIAGNOSTIC TOOLS

LISP provides a number of user-oriented tools for diagnosis of run-time errors, besides the normal system diagnostics. System-detected errors usually yield an error message related to the immediate cause of failure, followed by a short listing of the program flow leading to the immediate trapped function. The listing is called a "backtrace", and usually consists of the function names of the program hierarchy involved in the error. This information is gathered by the system as it "unwinds" the program hierarchy built up during evaluation, so as to reach the top level again. Some systems may also list the calling parameters of each function at the moment of error, and may even allow conditional user control of the unwinding process.

Some standard LISP diagnostic tools are listed below:

TRACE (L)   TRACE has one argument, L, a list of functions to be traced. After TRACE has been evaluated, the arguments, values, and name of each function are printed each time the function is entered and exited.

UNTRACE (L)   UNTRACE has one argument, L, a list of functions currently being traced. UNTRACE removes the tracing from all functions in list L.

GENSYM ( )   GENSYM has no arguments. Its value is a new, distinct, and freshly created literal atom with a print name (on most systems) of the form G00001, G00002, ..., G99999. This function is useful in debugging and general LISP programming for creating a literal atom when one is needed; each one is guaranteed to be unique. GENSYM names--if printed on cards, tape, or disc and subsequently read back into the system--will not correspond to an internal, existing GENSYM name. This is necessary to guarantee their uniqueness.

Other non-standard diagnostic tools, that allow even greater control of program execution are usually present in a given LISP system. These tools include user access to the error message and unwind control; conditional traps on CONS usage; and various breakpoint traps and traces. The literature for your system probably explains their operation and should be consulted.

17.3   INPUT-OUTPUT

Input and output in LISP are handled principally by the two pseudo-functions READ and PRINT, which read and print one S-expression, respectively. These functions are, in turn, defined in terms of more primitive machine-dependent functions. I have put together in this chapter a set of basic input-output functions that are representative of those found on most systems, even if their names and operations are not exactly those of your system.

READ ( )   READ is a pseudo-function of no arguments. Its evaluation
                causes the next S-expression to be read from the input
                device and structured internally as a LISP S-expression.
                All literal atoms seen by READ, which are already structured
                internally, are references to those structures. All new
                atoms (ones not seen before) cause new internal structures
                to be created as their reference. READ returns as its
                value the S-expression read. (The value, like all LISP
                values, is a pointer to the internal representation of
                the S-expression.)

PRINT (S)   PRINT is a pseudo-function of one argument, an S-expression.
                Its evaluation causes that S-expression to be printed on
                the output device and the argument to be returned as its
                value. Since the argument seen by PRINT is a pointer to
                the internal representation of the S-expression, PRINT
                computes a "print name" for the S-expression based upon
                the print names of all atoms in the S-expression and upon
                the structure of the S-expression. The print name of the
                S-expression is exactly the list notation used throughout
                this text. A definition of PRINT is given below. It
                uses primitives discussed in the next paragraph.

```
(PRINT (LAMBDA (X) (PROG ( )
   (PRIN X)
   (TERPRI)
   (RETURN X) )))

(PRIN (LAMBDA (X) (PROG (J)
   (COND ((ATOM X) (GO D)))
   (SETQ J X)
   (PRIN1 LPAR)
 A (PRIN (CAR J))
   (COND ((NULL (CDR J)) (GO C)))
   (PRIN1 BLANK)
   (COND ((ATOM (CDR J)) (GO B)))
```

```
                   (SETQ J (CDR J))
                   (GO A)
            B   (PRIN1 PERIOD)
                   (PRIN1 BLANK)
                   (PRIN1 (CDR J))
            C   (PRIN1 RPAR)
                   (RETURN X)
            D   (PRIN1 X)
                   (RETURN X) )))
```

The definition of PRIN above shows that PRIN is the work horse of PRINT. It
does the recursive computation for putting atom print names, left and right
parentheses, and "dots" into the print line. PRIN calls upon the primitive
PRIN1 to do the actual print line manipulations.

17.4   INPUT-OUTPUT PRIMITIVES

Most LISP systems use buffered I/O. The primitives listed here are responsible
for much of the internal I/O buffer management. The read line and print line
correspond to the internal buffers.

RATOM ( )   RATOM is a pseudo-function of no arguments used by READ.
                  Its evaluation causes the read line to be examined and
                  the characters therein to be parsed into an atom. If
                  the string of characters corresponds to number syntax, a
                  numerical atom is formed. If the character string obeys
                  literal atom syntax, a literal atom is formed. If neither,
                  an error results.

                  The value of RATOM is the atom read (i.e., the pointer to
                  the internal atomic structure) and the internal buffer
                  controls are advanced over the atom read. (In some systems,
                  RATOM is sufficiently flexible to allow knowledgeable users
                  to specify the syntax of atoms and thereby control the
                  parsing.)

READCH ( )   READCH is an invention for this text, but corresponds to
                  a pseudo-function of no arguments available on most systems.
                  (Some systems achieve the effect of READCH by flexible
                  control over RATOM.) Its evaluation causes the next
                  character in the read line to be returned as a literal
                  atom. No syntax check is made, hence all single characters
                  are acceptable literal atoms.

TEREAD ( )   TEREAD, meaning "TERminate READ", is a pseudo-function of
                  no arguments that clears the read line regardless of its
                  current contents. The value of TEREAD is NIL.

PRIN1 (A)   PRIN1 is a pseudo-function of one argument, an atom. Its
                  evaluation causes the internally stored print name of the
                  argument to be entered into the print line. The internal
                  buffer controls are advanced just beyond the atom printed.
                  The contents of the buffer are not normally transferred to
                  the output device, except when the buffer overflows. The
                  argument A must evaluate to an atom which is the value of
                  PRIN1.

TERPRI ( )   TERPRI, meaning "TERminate PRInt line", is a pseduo-
                  function of no arguments used by PRINT that dumps the
                  current print line on the external output device and then
                  clears the print line. A blank line is printed if the
                  print line is clear. The value of TERPRI is NIL.

17.5   THE OBLIST

RATOM is a machine-language routine that converts character strings into
internal atomic structure. When a non-numeric character string is read, it
must be compared with the character representation of all literal atoms seen
so far, to determine whether this string is a new atom or a reference to one
seen before.

There must be rapid access to all the atoms in the system. There exists, therefore, a list called the *object list*, or OBLIST, of all literal atoms. To speed
up the search for comparisons, the OBLIST is usually organized as a list of a
hundred or so sublists or "buckets". The atoms are distributed among the
buckets by a computation upon their Hollerith print names (hash coding), which
yields a reasonably uniform and random distribution of atoms among the buckets.

Thus, literal atoms in all LISP systems are unique, and have unique locations
(addresses) in the system. In some more recent systems, small numbers are
uniquely represented internally by the address resulting from adding a constant
displacement to their numerical values. The uniqueness of atoms permits rapid
testing for equivalent structures by EQ and EQUAL.

17.6   UNUSUALLY SPELLED LITERAL ATOMS

The syntax for literal atoms given in Chapter 2 notes that a literal atom is
any sequence of letters and digits, where the first character must be a letter.
We speak of such atoms as being "properly spelled", and now appreciate that
this spelling is the normal syntax accepted by RATOM.

Often, however, with extended character sets we wish to compose literal atoms
out of other than capital letters and digits. Such atoms are said to be
"unusually spelled". To use them, without modifying RATOM, we must use a string
quoting convention. Historically, this convention is called the *$$-artifact*.
We shall use and explain it here, even though more streamlined string quoting
apparatus exists on many current systems.

Any character string preceded by $$ will alert RATOM to the occurrence of an
unusually spelled literal atom. RATOM treats the character immediately follow-
ing the $$ as a "bracket" and then builds a literal atom out of all characters
preceding the next occurrence of the bracket character. The bracket character
may be any character. All characters between the "ad hoc" brackets will be
taken as the print name for a literal atom. Note that if the characters are
digits, no conversion takes place and the atom is literal, not numeric; i.e.,

$$EQUAL (\$\$*123* 123) = NIL$$

Some examples are shown below.

	$$-Artifact	Atom Formed	Bracket Character
1.	$$*NOW IS THE TIME*	NOW IS THE TIME	*
2.	$$$123$	123 (in Hollerith not binary)	$
3.	$$*ATOM*	ATOM	*
4.	$$B B	space	B
5.	$$.((.	((	.
6.	$$(..(	..	(

In example 3 above, $$*ATOM* is internally equivalent to the atom, ATOM. Thus, bindings for $$*ATOM* are bindings for ATOM; e.g.,

$$CSET\ (\$\$*ATOM*\ 123) = 123$$
$$(LAMBDA\ NIL\ ATOM)\ (\ ) = 123$$
$$EQUAL\ (\$\$*ATOM*\ ATOM) = T$$

17.7   CHARACTER OBJECTS

It is assumed here that every single character has a corresponding one-character literal atom already in the system. Thus, character "A" corresponds to the literal atom "A"; character "/" to the literal atom "/"; and character "7" to the literal atom "7". However, RATOM does not always read characters as literal atoms. It obeys the syntax of atoms that says literal atoms begin with a letter, etc. Thus, the character "7", if it were surrounded by blanks, would be read by RATOM or READ as a number, not as a literal atom. READCH, however, would read "7" as a literal atom. For RATOM or READ to read "7" as a literal atom, the $$-artifact must be employed; e.g., $$*7*.

An alternative to the $$-artifact is the use of *character objects*. A character object is a literal atom, the <u>value</u> of which is another literal atom with a special print name, that print name being some special character. The character object's print name is the English name for that character. The collection of character objects available depends upon the LISP implementation; however, the following are typical examples:

Character Object	Print Name of Value
LPAR	(
RPAR	)
BLANK	space
PERIOD	.
SLASH	/
EQSIGN	=
UPARROW	↑
DOLLAR	$
STAR	*
PLUSS	+
DASH	-

The user may define any others he may choose. For example,

CSET (COMMA $$*,*)[†]

binds the literal atom $$*,* as the value (i.e., the zero-level binding) of the literal atom COMMA. Then the value of COMMA will print as the character ",".

17.8   SUPERVISORS

In Paragraph 9.3 we examined the action of EVALQUOTE without being able at that time to examine its definition. We have now acquired all the necessary knowledge to define EVALQUOTE. This definition will work on all LISP systems, if the system can duplicate the function EVAL as defined in this text. In practice, EVALQUOTE requires more system housekeeping than is shown here; to give attention to system housekeeping chores, however, would not be germane to our discussion.

[†]Some LISP systems permit constants such as these to be defined by SET rather than, or in addition to, CSET.

```
(EVALQUOTE (LAMBDA ( ) (PROG (S1 S2 ARGS)
A       (TEREAD)
        (SETQ ARGS NIL)
        (SETQ S1 (READ))
        (SETQ S2 (READ))
B       (COND ((NULL S2) (GO C)))
        (SETQ ARGS (CONS (LIST (QUOTE QUOTE) (CAR S2)) ARGS))
        (SETQ S2 (CDR S2))
        (GO B)
C       (PRINT (EVAL (CONS S1 (REVERSE ARGS))))
        (GO A) )))
```

This function has no arguments and no value. It picks up its parameters and returns its value by doing explicit I/O with READ and PRINT. The program variables S1 and S2 are bound to the values of the two READ calls. These values are exactly the s_1 and s_2 pairs for EVALQUOTE described earlier in the text. For example,

$$\underbrace{\text{FOO}}_{s_1} \quad \underbrace{\text{(A B C)}}_{s_2}$$

The binding of ARGS (just below statement B) is the key to the program. It builds a list in which each element of S2 is quoted. For the above example, it builds the list

$$((\text{QUOTE C}) \ (\text{QUOTE B}) \ (\text{QUOTE A}))$$

adding one quoted element for each loop iteration. The iteration is terminated by the COND when the repeated CDR of S2 results in S2 being NIL. At that point we transfer to statement C and evaluate a computed form. The computed form for the example above is

$$(\text{FOO (QUOTE A) (QUOTE B) (QUOTE C)})$$

Note how the form is computed. The list bound to ARGS is reversed to properly order the quoted arguments. Then the value of S1, the function to be applied, is inserted at the head of the reversed list by CONS. This computed form is evaluated by EVAL, the value is printed by PRINT, and control transfers to statement A.

At statement A we do a TEREAD to clear the read line and re-initialize ARGS. It is this initial TEREAD that permits us to enter at the top level many right parentheses to balance the EVALQUOTE pair without counting. It also accounts for the inability to evaluate more than one EVALQUOTE pair per line.

The program definition appears to be in error because it will loop continuously. It is not an error, as we wish the supervisor to loop continuously, evaluating one EVALQUOTE pair for each iteration. That is what the supervisory program is supposed to do.

Another kind of supervisor not normally found at the top level of most LISP systems is one that will evaluate forms. Using EVAL, SUP3 will do just that.

```
DEFINE ((
    (SUP3 (LAMBDA ( ) (PROG ( )
    TAG1 (TEREAD)
          (PRINT (EVAL (READ)))
          (GO TAG1)))) ))
```

We can now comprehend some straightforward but unexpected top-level phenomena caused by the operation of EVALQUOTE, the top-level supervisor.

1. Composition of forms cannot be used directly at the top level except within a lambda expression. For example, if we write

    (CAR (QUOTE (A B C)))

    we do not have a _pair_ of S-expressions for EVALQUOTE. We could evaluate this form with our SUP3 supervisor, however.

2. Bound variables are never evaluated at the top level except within a lambda expression, because all arguments are quoted, e.g.,

    CSET (PI 3.14159)
    CAR ((PI)) = PI

    The result is PI, not 3.14159, since the argument of CAR really is (QUOTE (PI)). But

-132-

$$\text{(LAMBDA NIL PI) NIL} = 3.14159$$

since here PI is used free and will be evaluated. This is why top-level lambda expressions are so important.

3. If more than one pair of S-expressions is presented to EVALQUOTE, only the first pair of S-expressions will be evaluated by some systems; e.g.,

$$\text{CAR ((A B C)) CDR ((A B C))}$$

yields A. The CDR expression might not be seen by EVALQUOTE.

For systems that behave this way, the user may end a top-level expression with more right parentheses than are necessary, as EVALQUOTE stops reading as soon as the parentheses count out correctly in the second argument. For example,

$$\text{CAR ((A B C))))))))))))) } = \text{A}$$

4. If less than one pair of S-expressions is given to EVALQUOTE, it will demand more input. This is a useful debugging tool and usually means one or more right parentheses are missing in the entered pair of expressions.

5. An expression evaluated at the top level that explicitly PRINTS its value may have the value of the expression output twice--once by the explicit call to PRINT, and once by EVALQUOTE, which always prints the value of the expression, e.g.,

$$\text{PRINT (ABCD)}$$

yields

        ABCD
        ABCD

17.9   <u>EXERCISES</u>

Some of these exercises require an interactive LISP in which the user in on-line with the computer.

Evaluate the following in order:

1. PRINT ((LIST))

2. TERPRI NIL
    TERPRI NIL

3. (LAMBDA (X Y) (PROG ( )
           (PRIN1 X) (PRIN1 BLANK) (PRIN1 Y) (TERPRI))) (ATOM1 ATOM2)

4. READ NIL
    then enter:
    (NOW HEAR THIS)

5. (LAMBDA (J) (CONS (READ) J)) ((ANYTHING))
    then enter:
    (INPUT)

6. (LAMBDA NIL (PROG (PI R)
         (SETQ PI 3.14159)
    TAG (SETQ R (READ))
         (COND ((EQUAL (QUOTE END) R) (RETURN R)))
         (PRINT (TIMES 2 PI R))
         (GO TAG))) NIL
    Enter a number for R. The program returns the computation of
    2 * PI * R and then reads again.

    You can stop the loop by entering

              END

7. (LAMBDA ( ) (LIST LPAR RPAR BLANK PERIOD SLASH EQSIGN DOLLAR STAR
                  (QUOTE $$* NOW HEAR THIS *) (QUOTE $$+ -533.17+))) ( )

8. CDR ((A B C)) CDR ((1 2 3)) entered on one line.

9. 1. CSET(PERCENT $$*%*)

    2. (LAMBDA ( ) PERCENT) ( )

    3. (LAMBDA (J) J) (PERCENT)

10. CAR ((A B C))))))))))))))

11. Define EVALQUOTE given in the text as SUP2 to avoid a name clash
    with a possible EVALQUOTE in your system. Try SUP2 with these cases:

    SUP2() - - - - - - - - - - -to start SUP2 looping

    1. CAR ((A B C))

    2. CDR ((A B C))

    3. CONS (A B)

    4. CSET (PI 3.14159)

    5. (LAMBDA () PI) ( )

12. Define SUP3 as given earlier and try it with these cases:

    SUP3()

    1. (CAR (LIST (QUOTE (A))))

    2. (CONS (QUOTE A) (QUOTE B))

    3. (CSETQ K 3.14159)

    4. (CONS K NIL)

    5. (PROG (X) (PRIN1 (QUOTE X))
            (PRIN1 $$*   *) (PRIN1 (QUOTE SQUARE)) (TERPRI) (TERPRI)
            (SETQ X O)
        TAG1 (COND ((EQUAL X 10) (RETURN (QUOTE END))))
            (PRIN1 X) (PRIN1 $$*   *) (PRIN1 (TIMES X X)) (TERPRI)
            (SETQ X (ADD1 X))
            (GO TAG1))

13. Define SUP4, a supervisor that reads S-expression pairs in reverse
    order from that accepted by EVALQUOTE, i.e., s_2 followed by s_1.
    Try these pairs:

    1. ((A B C)) CAR

    2. ((A B C)) CDR

    3. (A B) EQ

    4. (1 2 3 4) PLUS

5. (K 3.14159) CSET

6. NIL (LAMBDA () K)

14. Define SUP5, a supervisor that evaluates pairs like SUP2, but also:

1. Saves the symbolic pairs.

2. Prints the pair for inspection after input, like an echo.

3. Queries your acceptance or rejection of the printed pair.

4. If you answer NO, it loops for another pair.

5. If you answer YES, SUP5 prints the pair, followed by an equal sign, followed by the value of the pair, and then loops for another pair.

15. Write a program that prints a table of the following values for a range of X specified at program run time.

X XSQUARE SQRTX RECIPX FACTORIALX

CHAPTER 18.
FUNCTIONAL ARGUMENTS

Mathematically, it is possible to have functions as arguments of other functions. For example, in arithmetic one could define a function

$$\text{OPERATE (op a b)}$$

where op is a functional argument that specifies which arithmetic operation is to be performed on a and b. Thus,

$$\text{OPERATE (+ 3 4) = 7}$$
$$\text{OPERATE (* 3 4) = 12}$$

In LISP, functional arguments are extremely useful and further expand the class of LISP functions. We call the class of functions that take this type of argument *functionals*.

18.1   FUNCTION

When arguments are transmitted to a function, they are always evaluated, except when they are transmitted to a special form which controls how its arguments are evaluated. When we use functions or functional expressions as arguments, we wish to transmit these arguments unevaluated. The special form FUNCTION is used for this purpose in LISP. FUNCTION acts very much like QUOTE, and in fact in some LISP systems, FUNCTION and QUOTE are often interchangeable. FUNCTION is used with functional arguments to signal that a function is being transmitted as an argument.

FUNCTION is a special form that takes one argument, a function name or a lambda expression. It has the form

$$\text{(FUNCTION } fexp)$$

where *fexp* is either the name of a function, or is a lambda expression.

We can see the application of functionals by examining a particularly powerful class of functions prefixed with the name MAP. These functions are generally alike, in that they all apply a functional argument to a list.

18.2   MAP

MAP is a function of two arguments of the form

MAP (X FN)

where the first argument, X, must be a list, and the second argument, FN, must be a function of one argument. MAP applies the function FN to list X and to successive CDR segments of the list X, until X is reduced to a single atom (usually NIL) which is returned as the value of MAP. MAP is defined by

```
DEFINE ((
  (MAP (LAMBDA (X FN) (PROG ( )
TAG1 (COND ((ATOM X) (RETURN X)))
     (FN X)
     (SETQ X (CDR X))
     (GO TAG1) ))) ))
```

Example:

(LAMBDA (L) (MAP L (FUNCTION PRINT))) ((THIS IS (A LIST)))

yields

```
(THIS IS (A LIST))
(IS (A LIST))
((A LIST))
NIL
```

In this example, PRINT is the functional argument. Each line of output represents the application of PRINT to successive CDR segments of the list (THIS IS (A LIST)). The final NIL is the value of MAP.

18.3   MAPLIST

MAPLIST is a function that performs almost exactly as does MAP, except MAPLIST returns as its value a list of the values of the repeated evaluation of FN applied to X

MAPLIST is a function of two arguments of the form

MAPLIST (X FN)

where the first argument, X, must be a list, and the second argument, FN, must be a function of one argument. The value of MAPLIST is a new list of the values of FN applied to the successive CDR segments of list X. That is, the value of MAPLIST (X FN) can be expressed as the value of the form

(LIST (FN X) (FN (CDR X)) (FN (CDDR X)) ... (FN (CD...DR X)))

A definition for MAPLIST can be given as

DEFINE ((
(MAPLIST (LAMBDA (X FN)
  (COND ((NULL X) NIL)
        (T (CONS (FN X) (MAPLIST (CDR X) FN))))))))

Examples:

DEFINE ((
(SQUARECAR (LAMBDA (X) (TIMES (CAR X) (CAR X))))))

(LAMBDA (J) (MAPLIST J (FUNCTION SQUARECAR))) ((1 2 3 4 5)) = (1 4 9 16 25)

(LAMBDA (J) (MAPLIST J (FUNCTION CDR))) ((A B C)) = ((B C) (C) NIL)

In these examples, SQUARECAR and CDR are functional arguments.

18.4   MAPCAR

The function MAPCAR is a function like MAPLIST, in that it lists the values of functional argument FN successively applied to each element of list X. It differs from MAPLIST, in that it applies FN to each element of the list X; i.e., the CAR of what FN is applied to in MAPLIST. MAPCAR is defined by

```
                    DEFINE ((

                  (MAPCAR (LAMBDA (X FN)

                    (COND ((NULL X) NIL)

                            (T (CONS (FN (CAR X)) (MAPCAR (CDR X) FN)))))) ))
```

Examples:

```
        (LAMBDA (J) (MAPCAR J (FUNCTION ADD1))) ((0 1 2 3)) = (1 2 3 4)   [1]

        (LAMBDA (J) (MAPCAR J (FUNCTION (LAMBDA (L)                       [2]
            (COND ((NUMBERP L) (TIMES L L))
                (T L)))))) ((A 1 B 2 C 3)) = (A 1 B 4 C 9)
```

In example [1], ADD1 is the functional argument, and the lambda expression adds
one to each element in a list of numbers. In example [2], we have a lambda expression as the functional argument. The result is the input list with each numerical
element replaced by its square.

18.5   MAPC

MAPC is a function of two arguments of the form

```
            MAPC (X FN)
```

where X is a list and FN is a function of one argument. MAPC is like MAPCAR
in its effect, but like MAP in its value. MAPC applies FN to each element of X,
and returns as its value the terminal element of the S-expression X (usually NIL).
It is defined by

```
                    DEFINE ((
                  (MAPC (LAMBDA (X FN) (PROG ( )
            A     (COND ((ATOM X) (RETURN X)))
                    (FN (CAR X))
                    (SETQ X (CDR X))
                    (GO A) ))) ))
```

Example:

                    (LAMBDA (L) (MAPC L (FUNCTION PRINT))) ((THIS IS (A LIST)))

yields

            THIS

            IS

            (A LIST)

            NIL

18.6   CAUTIONS

Most functionals (i.e., functions that take functional arguments) cannot be used
at the top level, since the special form FUNCTION must be evaluated. As we
know, EVALQUOTE quotes arguments when transmitting them, thus FUNCTION would not
be evaluated. Therefore, use functionals only in lambda expressions.

18.7   EXERCISES

Evaluate the following:

1. (LAMBDA (L) (MAP L (FUNCTION PRINT))) ((TRY THIS SIMPLE CASE FIRST))

2. (LAMBDA (L) (MAPC L (FUNCTION PRINT))) ((NOW THIS ONE))

3. (LAMBDA (L) (MAPCAR L (FUNCTION PRINT))) ((AND LASTLY THIS ONE))

4. (LAMBDA (J) (MAPLIST J (FUNCTION
        (LAMBDA (K) (SUBST[†] (QUOTE ONE) 1 K))))) ((1 2 3 1 4 1 5))

5. (LAMBDA (J) (MAPLIST J (FUNCTION
        (LAMBDA (K) (MAPCAR K (FUNCTION LENGTH))))))
        (((A) (1 2) (A B C) (1 2 3 4)))

6. (LAMBDA (L) (MAPLIST L (FUNCTION (LAMBDA (J) (CONS (CAR J)
        (CAR J)))))) ((A B C D E))

7. (LAMBDA (L) (MAPCAR L (FUNCTION (LAMBDA (J)
        (CONS J (QUOTE X)))))) ((A B C D E))

[†]SUBST is a built-in system function equivalent to function REPLACE, given as
exercise 20 of Chapter 14.

8. SPECIAL ((Y))
    DEFINE ((
      (YDOT (LAMBDA (L Y) (MAPCAR L (FUNCTION (LAMBDA (J)
        (CONS J Y))))))))
    UNSPECIAL ((Y))

Note:

> If we consider the functional argument here as a
> separate function, it is evident that it contains
> a bound variable J, and a free variable Y. This
> free variable requires a SPECIAL declaration, even
> though it is bound in YDOT.

Try

> YDOT ((A B C D E) Z)
>
> YDOT ((A B C D E) (1 2 3 4 5))

9. MAPCAR is a function of two arguments in which the second argument is
    a function that takes one argument. Define functional MAPCAR2 as a
    function of _three_ arguments in which the first two arguments are lists
    of equal length and the last argument is a function that takes _two_
    arguments; e.g.,

    (LAMBDA (A B) (MAPCAR2 A B (FUNCTION DIFFERENCE))) ((5 6 7 8) (1 2 3 4))
        = (4 4 4 4)

    (LAMBDA (A B) (MAPCAR2 A B (FUNCTION CONS))) ((ONE TWO THREE) (1 2 3))
        = ((ONE . 1) (TWO . 2) (THREE . 3))

10. Define a function using functionals called

        TYPE (x)

    where x is a list of items. The value of TYPE is a list of type-
    descriptors of each top-level element of x according to the following
    schedule:

if fixed-point number, FIX

if floating-point number, FLT

if literal atom, ATOM

if dotted pair of atoms, DOTPAIR

if none of the above, LIST

For example,

TYPE ((1.0 (A . B) (1 2 3) A12 46)) = (FLT DOTPAIR LIST ATOM FIX)

CHAPTER 19.

LIST STRUCTURES, PROPERTY LISTS, AND MACROS

Previous chapters of this text have discussed how computation may be performed with symbolic expressions. This chapter completes the discussion by focusing on additional features of LISP for manipulating and using list structures, property lists, and macros.

19.1 GRAPHICAL REPRESENTATION OF LIST STRUCTURE

In Chapter 3 we noted that the graphs of lists were in the form of binary trees. List structure is also of that form. Rather than representing the graph in a vertical format, however, it is conventional to represent the graph in a horizontal format that displays more clearly the level of sublists. For example, the list

(A B C)

was shown as the vertical graph

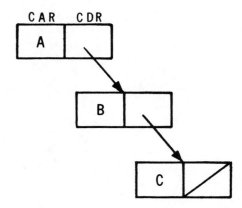

The entirely equivalent horizontal graph is given by

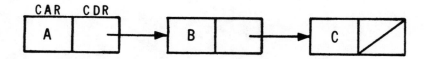

Similarly, the list

$$((A) \ (B) \ (C))$$

is the graph

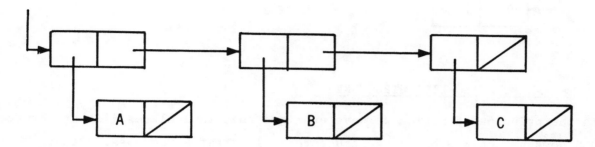

List structure in LISP is completely general and may be twisted, knotted, threaded, re-entrant or circular as the user desires. For example,

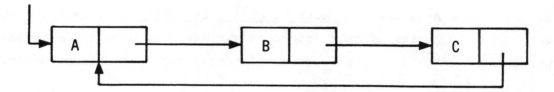

is the graph of a circular list (i.e., the tail points back to the head) that can occur in LISP as the result of computation. Of course, its printed representation is infinite in length, and is of the form

$$(A \ B \ C \ A \ B \ C \ A \ \dots)$$

Unless the LISP system provides special input-output mechanisms, such structures cannot be read or printed; however, they are perfectly proper structures and may find useful application.

Another interesting list structure is one that references a common sub-expression. For example, the S-expression

$$((JOHN \ . \ DOE) \ MARY \ (JOHN \ . \ DOE))$$

might represent the graph

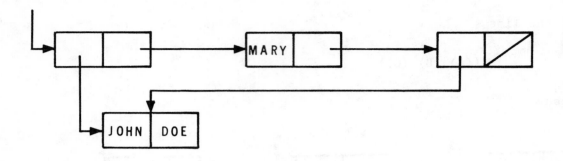

19.2   MANIPULATING LIST STRUCTURE

CONS is the principal function we have examined that manipulates list structure;
but CONS does not change existing structures: it creates new ones. Other
functions already treated, such as APPEND and SUBST, do not change structures,
but make modifications by copying their arguments. Copying is costly and in-
convenient. Complete generality in manipulating list structure is provided in
LISP by means of the pseudo-functions RPLACA and RPLACD, which change list
structure permanently. As such, they must be used with caution. They can cause
permanent damage to the system if used incorrectly. They may also cause infinite
search or printing of circular lists created unintentionally. Functions useful
for manipulating list structures are given below:

RPLACA (X Y)   RPLACA replaces the CAR of X by Y. Its value is X, but
                      X is now a different structure from what it was before.
                      The value of RPLACA can be described by the value of the
                      form

                         (CONS Y (CDR X))

                      However, the effect is quite different; there is no CONS
                      involved, only pointers are changed.

RPLACD (X Y)   RPLACD replaces the CDR of X by Y. Its value is X, but
                      X is now a different structure from what it was before.
                      The value of RPLACD can be described by the value of the
                      form

                         (CONS (CAR X) Y)

However, the effect is quite different; there is no CONS involved, only pointers are changed.

NCONC (X Y)   This function is similar to APPEND in effect. But NCONC does not copy list structure; it achieves the effect by modifying the list structure X, and making the last element of the structure point to the list Y. The value of NCONC is the list X, but since X has been modified, the value is the concatenated list of X and Y.

19.3   EXAMPLES OF MODIFYING LIST STRUCTURE

Assume the variables X and Y are bound to the lists (A B C) and (D E F), respectively. These lists have the graphs

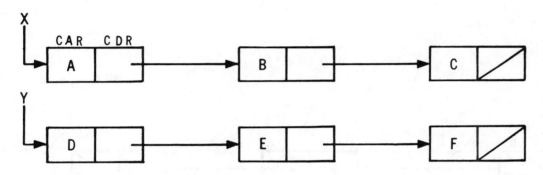

Evaluating the form

(RPLACA X Y)

yields the graph

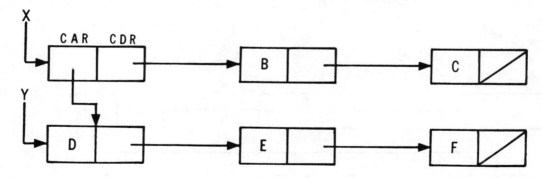

Evaluating the form

(RPLACD X Y)

yields the graph

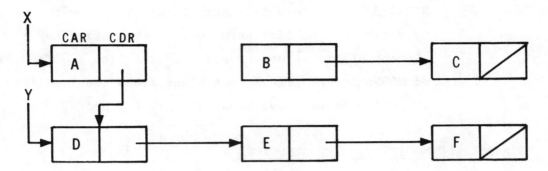

with the old CDR (X), i.e., list (B C), removed from the new structure.

Evaluating the form

(RPLACA X (CDR X))

yields the graph

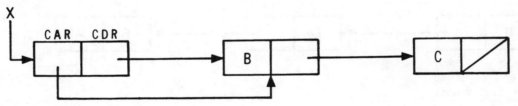

Evaluating the form

(NCONC X Y)

yields the graph

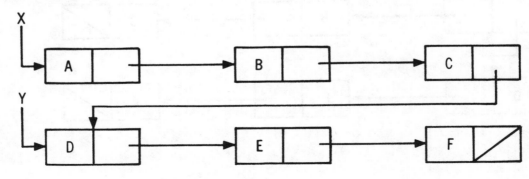

Evaluating the form

$$(NCONC\ X\ X)$$

yields the circular list

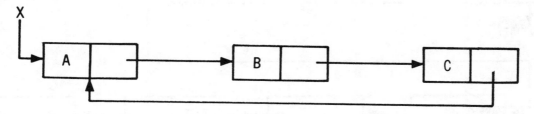

19.4   PROPERTY LISTS

What is the best way to organize a highly structured, yet indefinite collection of properties for a group of mathematical objects--a restricted dictionary of English words, for example? One simple solution is to have the data organized like an a-list, i.e., a list of pairs. One element of each pair could be a literal atom that represents the mathematical object; the other element of the pair could be the list of properties. Then functions like ASSOC could be used to search the list for desired information, using the literal atoms as indices.

An alternative solution is to directly "attach" the properties of interest to each atom. The attachment is achieved by means of a *property list* or *p-list* that is associated with each literal atom. For many applications, the use of property lists often improves the speed and flexibility of problem solution by replacing costly list searches with dictionary-like lookup on the property list.

For most LISP systems, literal atoms are represented internally in memory as list structures. Part of the structure is the BCD array for the print name of the atom; another part is the value cell for holding variable bindings. Other parts may be used by the system. Usually, the "CDR chain" of the structure is the property list.

The property list is provided for the user and is initially empty. (Some LISP systems use the property list for system features and it may have initial preset information.) Inasmuch as the property list is a general list, it may be used in any manner desired. However, a collection of system functions is available for manipulating property lists.

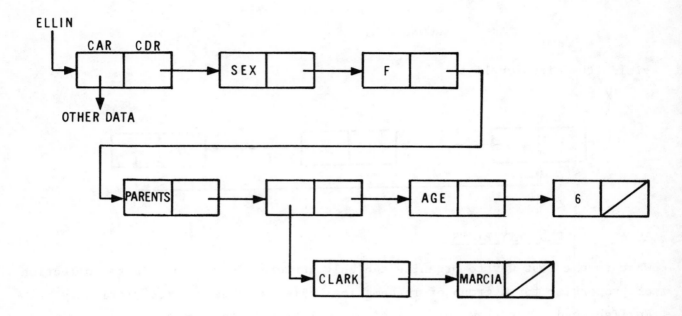

Before we examine the property list functions, note the atomic structure displayed above for the literal atom ELLIN. The property list "hangs" from the CDR of the structure. This is the convention adopted here and one that is similar to many LISP implementations. The property list is structured as a list of alternating indicators and properties; e.g., (SEX F PARENTS (CLARK MARCIA) AGE 6). Indicators[†] and properties are general S-expressions.

Several property list functions and their definitions are given below:

GET (X Y)   GET is a function that searches the list X for an indicator EQUAL[†] to Y. If such an indicator is found, its property--the next list element (i.e., the CAR of the rest of the list)--is returned as the value of GET. Otherwise, the value of GET is NIL.

PUT (X Y Z)   This function puts on the property list of the literal atom X the indicator Y followed by the property Z. Any previous property of Y is replaced by Z. The value of PUT is Y.

[†]Some systems use EQ rather than EQUAL in property list search functions, thereby requiring literal atoms as indicators.

PROP (X Y FN)   The function PROP searches the list X for an indicator
                 EQUAL[†] to Y. If such an indicator is found, the value
                 of PROP is the rest of the list beginning immediately
                 after that indicator. Otherwise, the value is FN ( ),
                 where FN is a function of no arguments.

REMPROP (X Y)   This function removes all occurrences of the indicator
                 Y and its property from the property list X. The
                 value of REMPROP is NIL.

19.5   EXAMPLES OF PROPERTY LIST FUNCTIONS

Assume the property list for ELLIN given in Paragraph 19.4. We may evaluate the
following expressions:

$$(GET \ (QUOTE \ ELLIN) \ (QUOTE \ AGE)) = 6$$
$$(LAMBDA \ (X \ Y) \ (PROP \ X \ Y \ (FUNCTION \ (LAMBDA \ (\ ) \ NIL))))$$
$$(ELLIN \ PARENTS) = ((CLARK \ MARCIA) \ AGE \ 6)$$
$$(LAMBDA \ (X \ Y \ Z) \ (PUT \ X \ Y \ Z))$$
$$(ELLIN \ SISTERS \ (HILLARY \ WENDY)) = SISTERS$$

After evaluation of this last example, the property list of ELLIN is augmented
by the indicator SISTERS and the property (HILLARY WENDY).

$$(REMPROP \ (QUOTE \ ELLIN) \ (QUOTE \ SEX)) = NIL$$

The result of this form is the deletion of the indicator SEX and the
property F from the p-list ELLIN.

19.6   MACROS

In a compiler-based LISP system, we must be concerned with both compile-time and
run-time activities of the system. When EVALQUOTE evaluates DEFINE, we are talking
about run-time for the pseudo-function DEFINE. If we are defining a function,
for example, LAST, we are talking about compile-time for LAST. In other words,
one function's run-time is another function's compile-time.

[†]Some systems use EQ rather than EQUAL in property list search functions, thereby
 requiring literal atoms as indicators.

As we have already seen, functions can be compiled by DEFINE or by top-level evaluation of a lambda expression. In the latter case, evaluation means first compile and then run the compiled code with the supplied arguments. This is often called "compiling at run-time". This distinction is significant because it enables compiled code to operate where previously an interpreter was necessary. In particular, it affects the code that is compiled for a function that enables that function to retrieve the correct binding for variables at run-time.

A classic problem for compilers is this: How do you define a function of an indefinite number of arguments, such as PLUS? The key to the answer is that the arguments are only indefinite when you define the function, not when you run it. If you could delay compilation until run-time, at which time the number of arguments is definite, you could resolve this dilemma. In essence, this is what an interpreter does. To resolve this problem in LISP, we make use of macros via the pseudo-function MACRO.[11]

19.7 MACRO EXPANSION

The function MACRO takes an argument list in the same format as DEFINE, e.g.,

$$MACRO ((\ (name_1\ (LAMBDA\ \mathit{varlist\ body}))$$
$$(name_2\ (LAMBDA\ \mathit{varlist\ body}))$$
$$.$$
$$.$$
$$.$$
$$(name_n\ (LAMBDA\ \mathit{varlist\ body}))\ ))$$

As with DEFINE, MACRO compiles each of these definitions. Now watch closely, for here comes the difference. When a macro function (defined by MACRO) is used in a lambda expression, either at the top level or within a DEFINE, the macro function is executed <u>before</u> the lambda expression (of which it is part) is compiled. The argument for the macro is the form in which it is used. In other words, the macro function is run before compile-time for its effect on the lambda expression. What does this buy us? That depends on the macro, but essentially it allows us to expand elements of the lambda expression before it is compiled, by substituting (for all occurrences of the macro function and its arguments) other expressions tailored to the particular use of the macro

-152-

in the lambda expression. We call this *macro expansion*. For example, it permits us to define a "special form" of an indefinite number of arguments by converting that special form to a composition of nested functions each having two arguments-- the nesting being determined by examination of the particular use of the special form in the given lambda expression.

Take, for example,

$$(PLUS\ x_1\ x_2\ \dots\ x_n)$$

Here we have a special form of an indefinite number of arguments. But when we use PLUS, we always have a fixed number of arguments. Given a function *PLUS, which takes the sum of its two arguments, we can expand

$$(PLUS\ x_1\ x_2\ x_3\ x_4) = (*PLUS\ x_1\ (*PLUS\ x_2\ (*PLUS\ x_3\ x_4)))$$

Thus, the macro definition of PLUS involves a body of code the sole purpose of which is to substitute *PLUS an appropriate number of times in the proper places wherever PLUS appears in a lambda expression being compiled. Then, after compilation, there is no trace of PLUS, but many occurrences of *PLUS. The operating code, however, works exactly as desired. Let's examine the macro definition for PLUS to see how this works.

```
            MACRO ((
            (PLUS (LAMBDA (L) (*EXPAND L (QUOTE *PLUS)))) ))
```

Here L, the argument for the macro PLUS, is the form

$$(PLUS\ x_1\ x_2\ x_3\ x_4)$$

*EXPAND is a system function used exclusively for expanding macros. It has the form

```
            (*EXPAND form fn)
```

where form is the expression to be expanded, as L above, and fn is the system function, a function of two arguments, to be used in the expansion. For

$$\text{form} = (\text{PLUS } x_1 \ x_2 \ x_3 \ x_4)$$

$$\text{fn} = *\text{PLUS}$$

we get

$$(*\text{EXPAND form fn}) = (*\text{PLUS } x_1 \ (\text{PLUS } x_2 \ x_3 \ x_4))$$

Note that *EXPAND just expands the form by one *PLUS when it is executed. When we then attempt to compile the new form

$$(*\text{PLUS } x_1 \ (\text{PLUS } x_2 \ x_3 \ x_4))$$

*EXPAND is called again to expand the inner PLUS,

$$\text{form} = (\text{PLUS } x_2 \ x_1 \ x_4)$$

$$\text{fn} = *\text{PLUS}$$

thereby yielding

$$(*\text{PLUS } x_1 \ (*\text{PLUS } x_2 \ (\text{PLUS } x_3 \ x_4)))$$

By repeated application of *EXPAND each time the macro PLUS is encountered, we eventually arrive at the complete expanded form for PLUS regardless of the number of arguments, x_n.

The definition for *EXPAND is straightforward and noted here for reference.

```
                DEFINE ((
                (*EXPAND (LAMBDA (FORM FN)
                   (COND ((NULL (CDDR FORM)) (CADR FORM))
                        (T (CONS FN
                                (CONS (CADR FORM)
                                (CONS (CONS (CAR FORM) (CDDR FORM)) NIL))))))) ))
```

Note how nicely *EXPAND works for the last term of the expansion

$$(*\text{PLUS } x_1 \ (*\text{PLUS } x_2 \ (*\text{PLUS } x_3 \ (\text{PLUS } x_4))))$$

When entered because macro PLUS was encountered,

$$\text{form} = (\text{PLUS } x_4)$$

$$\text{fn} = *\text{PLUS}$$

$$(\text{CDDR form}) = \text{NIL}$$

$$(\text{CADR form}) = x_4$$

Thus, the form

$$(\text{PLUS } x_4)$$

gets replaced by just x_4, yielding the final expanded expression

$$(*\text{PLUS } x_1 \; (*\text{PLUS } x_2 \; (*\text{PLUS } x_3 \; x_4)))$$

It should now be clear how elegant this macro system is. To solve the knotty problem of special forms of an indefinite number of arguments, all we need are four things:

1. *EXPAND--a single LISP function easily defined in LISP.

2. A function like the macro to be defined, but of just two arguments. Such a two-argument function is easily defined in LISP.

3. A macro definition of the special form.

4. MACRO recognition by the compiler.

Macros must be defined before they are used. Once defined, macros may be used within other macro definitions, thereby providing complete generality of MACRO. Since a macro must be defined before it can be used, macro definitions cannot be recursive; i.e., a macro cannot call itself.

19.8   <u>MACRO DEFINITIONS OF NEW FUNCTIONS</u>

MACRO has utility in areas other than expansion of special forms. It can be used to define functions not already in the system. Take, for example, the pseudo-function CSETQ. Assuming we have CSET, we can define CSETQ by

```
MACRO ((
  (CSETQ (LAMBDA (FORM) (LIST (QUOTE CSET)
                              (LIST (QUOTE QUOTE) (CADR FORM)) (CADDR FORM))))
        ))
```

Then whenever the form

$$(CSETQ \ A \ B)$$

is encountered,

$$(CSET \ (QUOTE \ A) \ B)$$

will be substituted and compiled.

19.9   <u>EXERCISES</u>

For the lists

$$X = ((CAT) \ (DOG) \ (FOX))$$

and

$$Y = (1 \ 2 \ 3.0)$$

evaluate the following forms; i.e., show the resulting graphs.

1. (NCONC X (NCONC X Y))

2. (RPLACD (RPLACA (CDR Y) (CONS (CADR Y) (CDDR Y))) NIL)

3. Define NCONC

4. Define the function REVLIST which reverses a list without copying.
    The effective value is like that returned by the function REVERSE.

5. A "blam" list is a list in which both the CAR and CDR point to the
    successor element of a list. (The list is useful for debugging the
    LISP garbage collector and for showing the generality of LISP list
    structure.) A three-element "blam" list has the graph

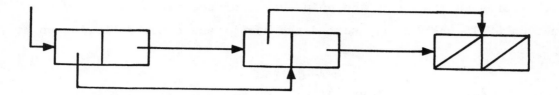

Define the BLAM function of one argument, a list, that modifies the list into a "blam" list. Do not use CONS.

Assume we are building a program to play contract bridge. The four players in the game are represented by the literal atoms NORTH, SOUTH, EAST, and WEST. The property list of each player has the indicator HAND and a list of 13 literal atoms (as the cards) for the property. Further assume each card has two indicators--SUIT and RANK--and the appropriate property for each. Use the properties SPADE, HEART, DIAMOND, and CLUB for the indicator SUIT, and the integers 14, 13, 12, etc. corresponding to Ace, King, Queen, etc. as the properties of the indicator RANK.

6. Define the function

        SUITS (player)

that: (1) separates the cards of a given hand into the four suits; (2) adds to the property list for that player the indicators SPADES, HEARTS, DIAMONDS, CLUBS and; (3) adds to the property list for that player the list of cards in each suit as the properties of these indicators.

7. Define the function

        LONGSUIT (player)

that returns as its value a dotted pair whose CAR is the name of the longest suit, and whose CDR is the length of that suit. Assume function SUITS above has already sorted the hand. For suits of equal maximum length, SPADES > HEARTS > DIAMONDS > CLUBS.

8. Define the function

        POINTS (player)

that returns as its value the point-count of the given hand. Assume function SUITS has already sorted the hand; assume the following point system:

Ace	(rank 14)	4 points
King	(rank 13) and suit length > 1	3 points
Queen	(rank 12) and suit length > 2	2 points
Jack	(rank 11) and suit length > 3	1 point
Void	(suit length = 0)	3 points
Singleton	(suit length = 1)	2 points

9. Define the predicate

    STOPPERS (player)

that is T if the hand contains <u>one</u> of the following combinations for <u>each</u> suit: ACE, or KING and length > 1, or QUEEN and length > 2; and NIL otherwise. Assume function SUITS has already sorted the hand.

10. Define the predicate

    BALANCED (player)

that is T if there are at least three cards in each suit of the hand, and NIL otherwise. Assume function SUITS has already sorted the hand. Use all your functions from problems 5-10 on an unsorted hand to define the function

    OPENBID (player)

that returns an opening bid in contract bridge according to the following schedule (with apologies to Charles Goren).

<u>Condition</u>	<u>Bid</u>
If points <13, and the longest suit <7 cards, then:	PASS
If 12 <points <20, and either stoppers = NIL, or balanced = NIL, where <suit> = longest suit, then:	(1 <suit>)
If 15 <points <20, and stoppers = T, and balanced = T, then:	(1 NO TRUMP)

If points >20, and either stoppers = NIL, or
balanced = NIL, where <suit> = longest suit, then: (2 <suit>)
If points >20, and stoppers = T, and
balanced = T, then: (2 NO TRUMP)
If 6 <points <13, and longest suit >6 cards,
where <suit> = longest suit, then: (3 <suit>)

11. *TIMES exists as a function of two arguments, the value of which is
     the product of its arguments. Define a macro function PROD, using
     *TIMES and *EXPAND such that

$$\text{PROD } (x_1\ x_2\ \ldots\ x_n) = (\text{*TIMES } x_1\ (\text{*TIMES } x_2\ \ldots\ (\text{*TIMES } x_{n-1}\ x_n)\ \ldots\ ))$$

12. *MAX and *MIN exist as functional counterparts of MAX and MIN, but
     having only two arguments. Define the macros MAXIMUM and MINIMUM.

13. In the last chapter, dealing with functional arguments, we saw that
     we must always use the special form FUNCTION, when we wish to quote a
     functional expression appearing as an argument of another functional
     expression; e.g.,

         (LAMBDA (L) (MAPLIST L (FUNCTION (LAMBDA (J) (LIST J)))))   [1]

Define the macro FLAMBDA, which when used as in form [2],

         (LAMBDA (L) (MAPLIST L (FLAMBDA (J) (LIST J))))   [2]

will expand form [2] to form [1].

14. If you define LIST as a macro and it's wrong, you can wreck the system.
     Therefore, define LIST1 as a macro that does exactly what LIST does.

Hint: Remember that

         $$(\text{CONS } x_{n-1}\ x_n) = (x_{n-1}\ \cdot\ x_n)$$

so the macro must produce

         $$(\text{CONS } x_n\ \text{NIL})$$

as its last expansion. In other words, we want

        LIST1 (A B C) = (A B C)

and <u>not</u>

        (A B . C)

15. When printing multi-word messages in LISP, we always print the
     message as a parenthetical expression, i.e., a list; e.g.,

            (NOW HEAR THIS)

     Define a macro PRINTQ that is a special form of an arbitrary number
     of arguments that quotes its arguments and prints them (on one line
     if they will fit) without parenthesization; e.g.,

            (LAMBDA ( ) (PRINTQ NOW HEAR THIS)) ( ) = NOW HEAR THIS

     Hint:

            Define PRINTQ as a macro that uses an auxiliary
            function PRINTQ1, which in turn uses PRIN on each
            argument of PRINTQ.

16. Paragraph 15.6 describes PROG2, a function of two arguments.
     Define the macro PROGN as a generalization of PROG2 for an
     indefinite number of arguments.

CHAPTER 20.
A COMPLETE LISP PROGRAM

In this concluding chapter we examine a collection of function definitions that constitute a LISP program which differentiates an algebraic polynomial. Assuming an on-line, interactive LISP system, the program reads the polynomial as an "infix" algebraic expression, and prints the derivative as an infix algebraic expression. The polynomial is constructed from the four arithmetic operators and exponentiation (with constant powers).

The treatment for other operators, such as logarithmic and trigonometric operators would not be significantly more difficult, but would require expanding the descriptive text without contributing more instructive material to the chapter. The formal syntax of the algebraic expression is listed below as a series of syntax equations in Backus Normal Form (BNF).[12] For those not familiar with this formal language for describing the syntax of formal languages, the English language interpretation of each equation is given.

20.1   POLYNOMIAL SYNTAX

Syntax Equation	English Interpretation
<digit> ::= 0|1|2|...|9	A *digit* is one of the ten numerals 0 to 9.
<variable> ::= A|B|C|...|Z	A *variable* is one of the 26 letters A to Z.
<constant> ::= <digit> <constant>|<digit>	A *constant* is an indefinite string of *digits*.
<mul> ::= *|<empty>	Multiplication is explicitly noted by the character "*", or implied by its absence.
<primary> ::= <variable>|<constant>|(<expression>)	A *primary* is either a *variable*, or a *constant*, or a parenthesized *expression*.

-161-

Syntax Equation	English Interpretation

<secondary> ::= <primary>↑<constant>|<primary>

> A *secondary* is either a *primary* raised to a *constant* power (explicitly noted by the character "↑"), or a *primary*.

<term> ::= <secondary>/<term>|<secondary> <mul> <term>|<secondary>

> A *term* is either a *secondary* divided by a *term* (explicitly noted by the character "/"), or a *secondary* (explicitly or implicitly multiplied by a *term*), or a *secondary*.

<expression> ::= <expression> + <term>|<expression> - <term>|<term>

> An *expression* is an indefinite sum or difference of *terms*.

These syntax equations allow implicit multiplication by limiting *variables* to one letter. They allow exponentiation to *constant* powers, and admit only integer *constants* of a magnitude within the computer's capacity. Though unary minus is excluded and the other operators are restricted to two operands, the remaining legal constructions allow for a rich set of algebraic *expressions*, some examples of which are noted below.

$$3X↑3 + 2X↑2 - X + 7$$
$$(A + B) (A - B)$$
$$3(A + B)↑3 + 2(A + B)↑2 + (A + B)$$
$$3↑27(A + B)↑2/A↑3 + (A/B)↑4$$

20.2   PROGRAM STRATEGY

The problem of symbolic differentiation in LISP is easily solved if the *expression* to be differentiated is represented as an S-expression in prefix notation. Some examples are shown below.

Infix Notation	S-Expression
A + B	(PLUS A B)
AX↑3 + BX↑2 − 3X	(PLUS (TIMES A (EXPT X 3))
	(DIFFERENCE (TIMES B (EXPT X 2))
	(TIMES 3 X)))

With this knowledge, the strategy is to translate the given *expression* into the desired prefix form, differentiate that form, and translate the resulting form back to infix notation. Though it is not obvious at this point, the solution also requires a program to perform algebraic simplification of the symbolic results of differentiation, and a supervisory program to control program execution and to perform input-output.

This overall strategy results in a complete LISP program structured as a hierarchy of sub-programs under the control of a supervisor program named DIFF. There are four principal sub-programs: IN2PRE, DERIV, SIMPLIFY, and PRE2IN. Each is a supervisor that controls further program hierarchies, and is itself a complete program. The balance of the chapter is devoted to describing these programs and their interaction with the supervisor DIFF.

20.3   IN2PRE

Many algorithms exist for translating from infix to prefix notation,[13,14] a technique well understood by compiler writers. The approach taken here, for its simplicity of exposition, is to use each of the BNF equations of Paragraph 20.1 as a basic specification for a LISP function. The set of functions defined satisfy the specifications of the syntax equations, and concurrently parse and translate the infix *expression*.

We have then, seven functions--DIGIT, VARIABLE, CONSTANT, PRIMARY, SECONDARY, and EXPRESSION--each corresponding to its like-named syntax equation. (We need only seven functions as the specification for *mul* can be subsumed by the function TERM.) There is also a function, NUMBER, that converts the indefinite string of *digits* collected by CONSTANT into a LISP number.

The function IN2PRE is a supervisory program that controls the translation and provides diagnostic information. It takes one argument, a list of all the non-blank characters, in order, from the infix *expression*. This list is supplied by the calling function DIFF.

Closer examination of the seven principal syntax equations shows that they only state whether a given string of characters satisfies the specification. In LISP, the seven corresponding functions can best accomplish this task if they are predicates. However, we want them to do more than just recognize legal syntax. We want them also to translate into prefix form that part of the input that satisfies the specifications, and to return the translation together with the untranslated portion of the input. If this is not enough of a problem, we also wish to avoid explicitly having to "backup" or restore the input string to its initial state when a given specification is not satisfied. We encounter this problem when the specification requires looking ahead into the string of characters before it can determine if the syntax equation is satisfied.

The solution to all these problems is to make the seven functions semi-predicates. Each of the seven functions, then, returns the value NIL (false) if the current state of the input does not satisfy the specifications of that function. If the specification is satisfied, the characters meeting the specifications are removed from the input list and replaced by their translated prefix form and the resulting list is returned as the value of the function (true). For example, if the function SECONDARY were called with the argument

$$(A \uparrow 3 + 7)$$

it would return the value

$$((\text{EXPT A } 3) + 7)$$

and since this value is non-NIL, it satisfies the conditional expression. The calling function--in this case TERM--knows that the CAR of the returned list is the translated *secondary*, and that the CDR is the remaining untranslated string of characters.

By using semi-predicates we satisfy the predicate nature of the syntax equations and simultaneously avoid explicit backup; backup being satisfied by properly binding and transmitting arguments between functions in the program hierarchy.

The complete listing of the function definitions for IN2PRE are given below. Note that the free variables DIGITS and ALPHA must be declared special before compilation of the functions DIGIT and CONSTANT, and that DIGITS and ALPHA must be bound before execution of IN2PRE. The proper bindings are given by:

CSET (DIGITS

(($$$0$ 0) ($$$1$ 1) ... ($$$9$ 9)))

CSET (ALPHA (A B C ... Z))

The reason for these bindings will become clearer after the discussion of the supervisor program DIFF.

```
(IN2PRE (LAMBDA (E)                                                      001
  (PROG (X)                                                              002
    (SETQ X (EXPRESSION E))                                             003
    (COND ((NULL X) (PRINT (QUOTE (POORLY FORMED EXPRESSION))))         004
          (T (RETURN X)))))))                                           005

(DIGIT (LAMBDA (E)                                                       006
  (PROG (X)                                                              007
    (SETQ X (ASSOC (CAR E) DIGITS))                                     008
    (COND ((NULL X) (RETURN NIL))                                       009
          (T (RETURN (CONS (CADR X) (CDR E)))))))))                     010

(VARIABLE (LAMBDA (E)                                                    011
    (COND ((MEMBER (CAR E) ALPHA) E)                                    012
          (T NIL))))                                                    013

(CONSTANT (LAMBDA (E)                                                    014
  (PROG (X Y)                                                           015
    (COND ((NULL (SETQ X (DIGIT E))) (RETURN NIL)))                     016
  A (SETQ Y (CONS (CAR X) Y))                                           017
    (SETQ E (CDR E))                                                    018
    (COND ((OR (NULL E) (NULL (SETQ X (DIGIT E))))                      019
            (RETURN (CONS (NUMBER (REVERSE Y)) E))))                    020
    (GO A))))                                                           021

(NUMBER (LAMBDA (E)                                                      022
  (PROG (X)                                                             023
    (SETQ X 0)                                                          024
  A (COND ((NULL E) (RETURN X)))                                        025
    (SETQ X (PLUS (TIMES X 10) (CAR E)))                                026
    (SETQ E (CDR E))                                                    027
    (GO A))))                                                           028

(PRIMARY (LAMBDA (E)                                                     029
  (PROG (X)                                                             030
    (COND ((SETQ X (VARIABLE E)) (RETURN X))                            031
          ((SETQ X (CONSTANT E)) (RETURN X))                            032
          ((NOT (EQ (CAR E) LPAR)) (RETURN NIL))                        033
          ((NOT (SETQ X (EXPRESSION (CDR E)))) (RETURN NIL))            034
          ((NULL (CDR X)) (RETURN NIL))                                 035
          ((EQ (CADR X) RPAR) (RETURN (CONS (CAR X) (CDDR X))))         036
          (T NIL))))))                                                  037
```

```
(SECONDARY (LAMBDA (E)                                                    038
  (PROG (X Y)                                                             039
    (COND ((NULL (SETQ X (PRIMARY E))) (RETURN NIL))                      040
          ((NULL (CDR X)) (RETURN X))                                     041
          ((NOT (EQ (CADR X) UPARROW)) (RETURN X))                        042
          ((SETQ Y (CONSTANT (CDDR X)))                                   043
             (RETURN (CONS (LIST (QUOTE EXPT) (CAR X) (CAR Y)) (CDR Y)))) 044
          (T (RETURN NIL))))))                                            045
(TERM (LAMBDA (E)                                                         046
  (PROG (X Y Z)                                                           047
    (SETQ X (SECONDARY E))                                                048
    (COND ((OR (NULL X) (NULL (CDR X))) (RETURN X)))                      049
    (SETQ Z (CDDR X))                                                     050
    (SETQ Y (QUOTE QUOTIENT))                                             051
    (COND ((EQ (CADR X) SLASH) (GO A)))                                   052
    (SETQ Y (QUOTE TIMES))                                                053
    (COND ((EQ (CADR X) STAR) (GO A)))                                    054
    (SETQ Z (CDR X))                                                      055
  A (COND ((SETQ Z (TERM Z))                                             056
             (RETURN (CONS (LIST Y (CAR X) (CAR Z)) (CDR Z))))            057
          (T (RETURN X))))))                                             058
(EXPRESSION (LAMBDA (E)                                                   059
  (PROG (EXP X Y OP)                                                      060
    (COND ((NULL E) (RETURN NIL))                                         061
          ((NULL (SETQ X (TERM E))) (RETURN NIL)))                        062
    (SETQ EXP (CAR X))                                                    063
  E (COND ((NULL (CDR X)) (RETURN EXP))                                   064
          ((EQ (CADR X) PLUSS) (SETQ OP (QUOTE PLUS)))                    065
          ((EQ (CADR X) DASH) (SETQ OP (QUOTE DIFFERENCE)))              066
          (T (RETURN (CONS EXP (CDR X)))))                                067
    (COND ((NULL (SETQ Y (TERM (CDDR X)))) (RETURN NIL)))                068
    (SETQ EXP (LIST OP EXP (CAR Y)))                                      069
    (SETQ X Y)                                                            070
    (GO E)))))                                                            071
```

20.4   <u>DERIV</u>

DERIV is a compact, recursive function that completely differentiates the prefix
expression returned by IN2PRE, with respect to a given *variable*. Listed below
are the seven necessary and sufficient differentiation rules satisfied by DERIV.
The line numbers to the right of each rule show the correspondence between the
rule and its coded form in the function DERIV listed below.

	Differentiation Rules	Line No.

1. $\dfrac{du}{dx} = 0$; if $u \neq f(x)$ 73

2. $\dfrac{du}{dx} = 1$; if $u = x$ 73

3. $\dfrac{d}{dx}(u + v) = \dfrac{du}{dx} + \dfrac{dv}{dx}$ 74

4. $\dfrac{d}{dx}(u - v) = \dfrac{du}{dx} - \dfrac{dv}{dx}$ 74

5. $\dfrac{d}{dx}(uv) = v\,\dfrac{du}{dx} + u\,\dfrac{dv}{dx}$ 76

6. $\dfrac{d}{dx}(u/v) = (v\,\dfrac{du}{dx} - u\,\dfrac{dv}{dx}) / v^2$ 80

7. $\dfrac{d}{dx}(u^n) = n\,u^{n-1}\,\dfrac{du}{dx}$; if $n = \mathit{constant}$ 86

```
(DERIV (LAMBDA (E X)                                                        072
   (COND ((ATOM E) (COND ((EQ E X) 1) (T 0)))                               073
         ((OR (EQ (CAR E) (QUOTE PLUS)) (EQ (CAR E) (QUOTE DIFFERENCE)))    074
          (LIST (CAR E) (DERIV (CADR E) X) (DERIV (CADDR E) X)))            075
         ((EQ (CAR E) (QUOTE TIMES))                                        076
          (LIST (QUOTE PLUS)                                                077
            (LIST (CAR E) (CADDR E) (DERIV (CADR E) X))                     078
            (LIST (CAR E) (CADR E) (DERIV (CADDR E) X))))                   079
         ((EQ (CAR E) (QUOTE QUOTIENT))                                     080
          (LIST (CAR E)                                                     081
            (LIST (QUOTE DIFFERENCE)                                        082
              (LIST (QUOTE TIMES) (CADDR E) (DERIV (CADR E) X))             083
              (LIST (QUOTE TIMES) (CADR E) (DERIV (CADDR E) X)))            084
            (LIST (QUOTE TIMES) (CADDR E) (CADDR E))))                      085
         ((EQ (CAR E) (QUOTE EXPT))                                         086
          (LIST (QUOTE TIMES)                                              087
            (LIST (QUOTE TIMES) (CADDR E)                                   088
              (COND ((EQUAL (CADDR E) 2) (CADR E))                          089
                    (T (LIST (CAR E) (CADR E) (SUB1 (CADDR E))))))          090
            (DERIV (CADR E) X)))                                            091
         (T NIL)))))                                                        092
```

The structure of the function DERIV is simple. It is one conditional expression with six conditional clauses; each clause satisfies one or two differentiation rules. Since the rules are determined by the arithmetic operation, and a non-atomic prefix *expression* always has the form

$$\text{(operator argument}_1 \text{ argument}_2)$$

the predicates in each clause determine if the given *expression* satisfies its rule by examining the *expression's* operator (the CAR of the *expression*.) (For atomic *expressions*, rules 1 and 2 are detected by the predicate ATOM.) If the predicate is true, the clause applies its rule by simple evaluation or by using recursive calls upon DERIV.

For example, if the original infix *expression* were

$$3X\uparrow2 + 2X$$

IN2PRE would return the prefix *expression*

$$\text{(PLUS (TIMES 3 (EXPT X 2)) (TIMES 2 X))}$$

for DERIV. If this *expression* is differentiated with respect to X, the second clause (line 74) would be satisfied, and rule 3 would be applied, yielding the *expression*

$$\text{(PLUS (DERIV argument}_1 \text{ X) (DERIV argument}_2 \text{ X))}$$

This *expression* is not completely evaluated. For

$$\text{argument}_1 = \text{(TIMES 3 (EXPT X 2))}$$
$$\text{argument}_2 = \text{(TIMES 2 X)}$$

the recursive call to DERIV, for each of these arguments, would invoke rule 5 (line 76), resulting in the incompletely evaluated *expressions*

$$\text{(PLUS (TIMES (EXPT X 2) (DERIV argument}_{11} \text{ X))}$$
$$\text{(TIMES 3 (DERIV argument}_{12} \text{ X)))}$$

and

$$\text{(PLUS (TIMES X (DERIV argument}_{21}\text{ X))}$$
$$\text{(TIMES 2 (DERIV argument}_{22}\text{ X)))}$$

Again, for

$$\text{argument}_{11} = 3, \qquad \text{argument}_{12} = \text{(EXPT X 2)}$$
$$\text{argument}_{21} = 2, \qquad \text{argument}_{22} = \text{X}$$

recursive calls to DERIV are required, invoking rules 1 and 2 (line 73) for arguments 11, 21, and 22, and rule 7 (line 86) for argument 12. DERIV yields a value of zero for arguments 11 and 21, one for argument 22, and

$$\text{(TIMES (TIMES 2 X) (DERIV argument}_{121}\text{ X))}$$

for argument 12.

The final recursive call to DERIV with

$$\text{argument}_{121} = \text{X}$$

invokes rule 2 and returns a value of one.

Thus, the complete symbolic differentiation yields the *expression*

$$\text{(PLUS (PLUS (TIMES (EXPT X 2) 0)}$$
$$\text{(TIMES 3 (TIMES (TIMES 2 X) 1)))}$$
$$\text{(PLUS (TIMES X 0) (TIMES 2 1)))}$$

When simplified, this *expression* is reduced to its algebraic equivalent

$$\text{(PLUS (TIMES 6 X) 2)}$$

or in infix notation

$$6X + 2$$

The need for algebraic simplification is obvious from this simple example. How we shall achieve simplification is the subject of the next function to be considered--SIMPLIFY.

20.5   <u>SIMPLIFY</u>

Arithmetic simplification of symbolic *expressions* is an art, and the subject of
many learned papers in the programming literature.[15,16]   I have used a straightforward approach, one that yields a simpler *expression*, but not necessarily
the simplest *expression*. This is because SIMPLIFY does not look for common
factors among the arguments of the various sub-*expressions*. It is also "blind"
to simplifications that are possible between arguments of adjacent nested
operators. However, it does satisfy a host of rules which simplify the majority
of *expressions* allowable in this problem.

The hardest part of this problem was determining which of a large number of
individual rules should be treated by SIMPLIFY. Brevity was my guiding light,
and yet SIMPLIFY is the largest of the five parts of the complete program.

SIMPLIFY is a supervisory program that parcels the task of simplification among
five sub-functions--SPLUS, STIMES, SQUOTIENT, SEXPT, and SMINUS--according to
the given arithmetic operator involved. There is no function SDIFFERENCE, since
SIMPLIFY transforms an *expression* of the form

> (DIFFERENCE a b)

into an *expression* of the form

> (PLUS (MINUS b) a)

The function SMINUS satisfies the simplification requirements of the unary
operator MINUS that is generated by SIMPLIFY. Unary MINUS is not a legal
operator in the construction of the input polynomial.

The hierarchical sub-functions called by SIMPLIFY all adhere to a number of
principles:

1. Each function assumes its arguments are in simplest form by earlier evaluation of SIMPLIFY on these arguments (lines 96 and 99).

2. *Expressions* with *constant* arguments are always simplified by arithmetic evaluation of the *expression* using EVAL.

3. Except for *constants*, MINUS is always factored out of the arguments of an *expression*.

4. SPLUS and STIMES always return their value in a standard form, i.e., the first argument is always the *constant*, if there is one.

5. The input *expression* is returned unchanged, if all simplification rules fail.

```
(SIMPLIFY (LAMBDA (E)                                        093
  (PROG (A B C D)                                            094
    (COND ((ATOM E) (RETURN E)))                             095
    (SETQ A (SIMPLIFY (CADR E)))                             096
    (COND ((EQ (SETQ C (CAR E)) (QUOTE MINUS))               097
           (RETURN (SMINUS (LIST C A)))))                    098
    (SETQ B (SIMPLIFY (CADDR E)))                            099
    (COND ((EQ C (QUOTE DIFFERENCE))                         100
           (RETURN (SPLUS (LIST (QUOTE PLUS)                 101
             (SMINUS (LIST (QUOTE MINUS) B)) A)))))          102
    (SETQ D (LIST C A B))                                    103
    (RETURN (SELECT C ((QUOTE PLUS) (SPLUS D))               104
                      ((QUOTE TIMES) (STIMES D))             105
                      ((QUOTE QUOTIENT) (SQUOTIENT D))       106
                      ((QUOTE EXPT) (SEXPT D))               107
                      D )))))                                108
```

20.5.1   SPLUS

For an *expression* of the form

(PLUS a b)

the following simplification rules are used by SPLUS. Higher-numbered rules assume prior rules failed.

	Rule	Value	Line No.
1.	a and b = *constant*	a + b	111
2.	a = 0	b	115
3.	b = 0	a	112
4.	b = *constant*, a ≠ *constant*	(PLUS b a)†	113
5.	a = b	(TIMES 2 a)†	116
6.	a = (MINUS a_1) b = (MINUS b_1)	(MINUS (PLUS a_1 b_1)†)	121
7.	a = (MINUS a_1), b = a_1	0	125
8.	a = (MINUS a_1), b ≠ *constant*	(PLUS b a)†	126
9.	b = (MINUS b_1), a = b_1	0	128
10.	b = (MINUS b_1), a ≠ *constant*	(PLUS a b)†	129
11.	all else	(PLUS a b)†	130

```
(SPLUS (LAMBDA (E)                                               109
  (COND ((NUMBERP (CADDR E))                                     110
          (COND ((NUMBERP (CADR E)) (EVAL E))                    111
                ((ZEROP (CADDR E)) (CADR E))                     112
                (T (COLLECT (LIST (CAR E) (CADDR E) (CADR E))))))  113
                                                                 114
        ((AND (NUMBERP (CADR E)) (ZEROP (CADR E))) (CADDR E))    115
        ((EQUAL (CADR E) (CADDR E))                              116
          (COLLECT (LIST (QUOTE TIMES) 2 (CADR E))))             117
        ((AND (NOT (ATOM (CADR E))) (EQ (CAADR E) (QUOTE MINUS)))  118
          (COND ((AND (NOT (ATOM (CADDR E)))                     119
                      (EQ (CAADDR E) (QUOTE MINUS)))             120
                  (LIST (QUOTE MINUS)                            121
                    (COLLECT (LIST (CAR E)                       122
                                   (CADADR E)                    123
                                   (CADR (CADDR E))))))          124
                ((EQUAL (CADADR E) (CADDR E)) 0)                 125
                (T (COLLECT (LIST (CAR E) (CADDR E) (CADR E)))))) 126
        ((AND (NOT (ATOM (CADDR E))) (EQ (CAADDR E) (QUOTE MINUS)))  127
          (COND ((EQUAL (CADR (CADDR E)) (CADR E)) 0)            128
                (T (COLLECT E))))                                129
        (T (COLLECT E)))))                                       130
```

---

†The *expression* is further simplified by the function COLLECT, which is described later.

-172-

20.5.2   STIMES

For an *expression* of the form

$$(\text{TIMES a b})$$

the following simplification rules are used by STIMES. Higher-numbered rules assume prior rules failed.

	Rule	Value	Line No.
1.	a and b = *constant*	a * b	133
2.	a = 0	0	138
3.	a = 1	b	139
4.	a = *constant*, b $\neq$ *constant*	(TIMES a b)[†]	140
5.	b = 0	0	134
6.	b = 1	a	135
7.	b = *constant*, a $\neq$ *constant*	(TIMES b a)[†]	136
8.	a = b	(EXPT a 2)[††]	141
9.	a = (MINUS a_1) b = (MINUS b_1)	(TIMES a_1 b_1)[†]	144
10.	a = (MINUS a_1), b = a_1	(MINUS (EXPT b 2))	147
11.	a = (MINUS a_1), b $\neq$ *constant*	(TIMES b a)[†]	149
12.	b = (MINUS b_1), a = b_1	(MINUS (EXPT a 2))	151
13.	b = (MINUS b_1), a $\neq$ *constant*	(TIMES a b)[†]	153
14.	all else	(TIMES a b)[†]	154

```
(STIMES (LAMBDA (E)                                                      131
    (COND ((NUMBERP (CADDR E))                                           132
            (COND ((NUMBERP (CADR E)) (EVAL E))                          133
                  ((ZEROP (CADDR E)) 0)                                  134
                  ((ONEP (CADDR E)) (CADR E))                            135
                  (T (COLLECT (LIST (CAR E) (CADDR E) (CADR E)))))))     136
          ((NUMBERP (CADR E))                                            137
            (COND ((ZEROP (CADR E)) 0)                                   138
                  ((ONEP (CADR E)) (CADDR E))                            139
                  (T (COLLECT E))))                                      140
          ((EQUAL (CADR E) (CADDR E))                                    141
            (SEXPT (LIST (QUOTE EXPT) (CADR E) 2)))                      142
          ((AND (NOT (ATOM (CADR E))) (EQ (CAADR E) (QUOTE MINUS)))      143
            (COND ((AND (NOT (ATOM (CADDR E)))                           144
                        (EQ (CAADDR E) (QUOTE MINUS)))                   145
                    (COLLECT (LIST (CAR E) (CADADR E) (CADR (CADDR E)))))  146
                  ((EQUAL (CADADR E) (CADDR E))                          147
                    (LIST (QUOTE MINUS) (LIST (QUOTE EXPT) (CADDR E) 2)))  148
                  (T (COLLECT (LIST (CAR E) (CADADR E) (CADR E)))))))    149
```

[†]The *expression* is further simplified by the function COLLECT, which is described later.

[††]The *expression* is further simplified by the function SEXPT, which is described later.

```
          ((AND (NOT (ATOM (CADDR E))) (EQ (CAADDR E) (QUOTE MINUS)))        150
              (COND ((EQUAL (CADR (CADDR E)) (CADR E))                       151
                    (LIST (QUOTE MINUS) (LIST (QUOTE EXPT) (CADR E) 2)))     152
                    (T (COLLECT E))))                                        153
          (T (COLLECT E)))))                                                 154
```

20.5.3   COLLECT

COLLECT is a function common to both SPLUS and STIMES. It provides additional simplification rules applicable to both functions. COLLECT attempts to simplify an *expression* if it matches various patterns of nested PLUS or TIMES operators.

	Rule	Value	Line No.
1.	*expression* = atom	*expression*	156
2.	*expression* = (operator a b)		
	a = atom, b = atom	(operator a b)	158
3.	*expression* = (operator a b)		
	a ≠ atom, b = atom	(operator b a)[†]	159
4.	(PLUS a (PLUS b c))		
	a and b = *constant*	(PLUS a + b c)	161
5.	(TIMES a (TIMES b c))		
	a and b = *constant*	(TIMES a * b c)	161
6.	(PLUS (PLUS a b) (PLUS c d))		
	a and c = *constant*	(PLUS a + c (PLUS b d))	166
7.	(TIMES (TIMES a b) (TIMES c d))		
	a and c = *constant*	(TIMES a * c (TIMES b d))	166
8.	all else	*expression*	171 and 172

```
(COLLECT (LAMBDA (E)                                                          155
    (COND ((ATOM E) E)                                                        156
          ((ATOM (CADDR E))                                                   157
           (COND ((ATOM (CADR E)) E)                                          158
                 (T (COLLECT (LIST (CAR E) (CADDR E) (CADR E))))))            159
          ((AND (EQ (CAR E) (CAADDR E)) (NUMBERP (CADR (CADDR E))))           160
           (COND ((NUMBERP (CADR E))                                          161
                  (LIST (CAR E)                                               162
                        (EVAL (LIST (CAR E) (CADR E) (CADR (CADDR E))))       163
                        (CADDR (CADDR E))))                                   164
                 ((ATOM (CADR E)) E)                                          165
                 ((AND (EQ (CAR E) (CAADR E)) (NUMBERP (CADADR E)))           166
                  (LIST (CAR E)                                               167
                        (EVAL (LIST (CAR E) (CADADR E) (CADR (CADDR E))))     168
                        (LIST (CAR E) (CADDR (CADR E))                        169
                              (CADDR (CADDR E)))))                            170
                 (T E)))                                                      171
          (T E)))))                                                          172
```

[†]The *expression* is further simplified by a recursive call to COLLECT.

20.5.4   SQUOTIENT

SQUOTIENT attempts some minor simplifications. If they fail, the form

$$(QUOTIENT\ a\ b)$$

is transformed into the form

$$(TIMES\ a\ (QUOTIENT\ 1\ b))$$

and a call to STIMES is made with the new *expression*. SQUOTIENT does not make a zero-divide check, i.e., b is assumed $\neq$ 0.

Rule	Value	Line No.
1. $a = b$	1	174
2. $a = 0$	0	175
3. $a = 1$	(QUOTIENT a b)	176
4. $b = 1$	a	179
5. a and b = *constant*	a/b	178
6. b = *constant*, a $\neq$ *constant*	(TIMES 1.0/b a)[†]	180
7. b = (MINUS b_1)	(TIMES a (MINUS (QUOTIENT 1 b_1)))[††]	182
8. all else	(TIMES a (QUOTIENT 1 b))[††]	187

```
(SQUOTIENT (LAMBDA (E)                                                  173
    (COND ((EQUAL (CADR E) (CADDR E)) 1)                                174
          ((AND (NUMBERP (CADR E)) (ZEROP (CADR E))) 0)                 175
          ((AND (NUMBERP (CADR E)) (ONEP (CADR E))) E)                  176
          ((NUMBERP (CADDR E))                                          177
           (COND ((NUMBERP (CADR E)) (EVAL E))                          178
                 ((ONEP (CADDR E)) (CADR E))                            179
                 (T (COLLECT (LIST (QUOTE TIMES)                        180
                             (QUOTIENT 1.0 (CADDR E)) (CADR E))))))     181
          ((AND (NOT (ATOM (CADDR E))) (EQ (CAADDR E) (QUOTE MINUS)))   182
           (STIMES (LIST (QUOTE TIMES) (CADR E)                         183
                   (LIST (QUOTE MINUS)                                  184
                         (LIST (QUOTE QUOTIENT)                         185
                               1 (CADR (CADDR E)))))))                  186
          (T (STIMES (LIST (QUOTE TIMES) (CADR E)                       187
                     (LIST (QUOTE QUOTIENT) 1 (CADDR E)))))))))         188
```

[†]The *expression* is further simplified by the function COLLECT.

[††]The *expression* is further simplified by the function STIMES.

20.5.5 SEXPT

For an *expression* of the form

$$(EXPT\ a\ b)$$

the following simplification rules are used by SEXPT. The argument b is assumed to be constant (i.e., NUMBERP is not used to guarantee this fact). 0^0 is defined equal to one.

Rule	Value	Line No.
1. $b = 0$	1	190
2. $b = 1$	a	191
3. a and b = *constant*	a^b	192
4. a = atom	(EXPT a b)	193
5. $a = (EXPT\ a_1\ b_1)$	$(EXPT\ a_1\ b\ *\ b_1)$	194
6. $a = (MINUS\ a_1)$, b = even	$(EXPT\ a_1\ b)$[†]	198
7. $a = (MINUS\ a_1)$, b = odd	$(MINUS\ (EXPT\ a_1\ b)$[†]$)$	200
8. all else	(EXPT a b)	197

```
(SEXPT (LAMBDA (E)                                                      189
    (COND ((ZEROP (CADDR E)) 1)                                         190
          ((ONEP (CADDR E)) (CADR E))                                   191
          ((NUMBERP (CADR E)) (EVAL E))                                 192
          ((ATOM (CADR E)) E)                                           193
          ((EQ (CAADR E) (QUOTE EXPT))                                  194
           (LIST (QUOTE EXPT) (CADADR E)                                195
                 (TIMES (CADDR E) (CADDR (CADR E)))))                   196
          ((NOT (EQ (CAADR E) (QUOTE MINUS))) E)                        197
          ((EVENP (CADDR E))                                            198
           (SEXPT (LIST (QUOTE EXPT) (CADADR E) (CADDR E))))            199
          (T (LIST (QUOTE MINUS)                                        200
                   (SEXPT (LIST (QUOTE EXPT) (CADADR E) (CADDR E))))))))) 201
```

20.5.6 SMINUS

The rules below apply to an *expression* of the form

$$(MINUS\ a)$$

[†]The *expression* is further simplified by a recursive call to SEXPT.

Rule	Value	Line No.
1. a = *constant*	-a	203
2. a = (MINUS a_1)	a_1	204
3. all else	(MINUS a)	206

```
(SMINUS (LAMBDA (E)                                           202
    (COND ((NUMBERP (CADR E)) (EVAL E))                       203
          ((AND (NOT (ATOM (CADR E)))                         204
                (EQ (CAADR E) (QUOTE MINUS))) (CADADR E))     205
          (T E)))))                                           206
```

20.6   PRE2IN

Translating from prefix to infix notation is considerably simpler than vice versa, and PRE2IN is a simpler function than IN2PRE. There are only two problems: (1) determining when to parenthesize an *expression* to remove ambiguity, and (2) printing the *expression* in a "pretty" infix form.

The first problem is solved by taking cognizance of the precedence or binding strength of adjacent operators. When printing an *expression* whose operator has higher precedence than the operator of an argument, the argument is parenthesized. For example, the *expression*

            (TIMES A (PLUS B C))

should print as

            A(B + C)

whereas

            (PLUS A (TIMES B C))

should print as

            A + BC

since TIMES has higher precedence than PLUS. For our problem, operator precedence, from high to low, is as listed below:

            EXPT
            TIMES, QUOTIENT
            PLUS, MINUS

-177-

where TIMES and QUOTIENT (and PLUS and MINUS) have equal precedence. The
function WRAP provides the parentheses when called.

The second problem of printing the *expression* in a "pretty" format is sidestepped
to some degree by PRE2IN, particularly for the case

$$(TIMES \ constant \ (QUOTIENT \ 1 \ A))$$

If the *constant* were 3, the infix *expression* could print as

$$31/A$$

which is incorrect. The solution I've chosen is to always insert a space
following a *constant* (line 209). A better printing algorithm could yield

$$3/A$$

but this is not done here.

The structure of PRE2IN includes the supervisory program PRE2IN and six sub-
functions. They are simple enough to be left to the reader to follow the
code directly. Note, however, the use of the character objects PLUSS, SLASH,
DASH, UPARROW, LPAR, RPAR, and BLANK, whose values print as the desired
characters.

```
(PRE2IN (LAMBDA (E)                                               207
  (PROG ()                                                        208
    (COND ((NUMBERP E) (PROG2 (PRIN E) (PRIN BLANK)))             209
          ((ATOM E) (PRIN E))                                     210
          (T (SELECT (CAR E)                                      211
                  ((QUOTE PLUS) (XPLUS E))                        212
                  ((QUOTE MINUS) (XMINUS E))                      213
                  ((QUOTE TIMES) (XTIMES E))                      214
                  ((QUOTE QUOTIENT) (XQUOTIENT E))                215
                  ((QUOTE EXPT) (XEXPT E)) E))))))                216

(XPLUS (LAMBDA (E)                                                217
  (PROG ()                                                        218
    (COND ((NUMBERP (CADR E))                                     219
            (RETURN (XPLUS (LIST (CAR E) (CADDR E) (CADR E))))))  220
    (PRE2IN (CADR E))                                             221
    (PRIN BLANK)                                                  222
    (COND ((AND (NOT (ATOM (CADDR E))) (EQ (CAADDR E) (QUOTE MINUS)))  223
            (GO X))                                               224
          ((AND (NUMBERP (CADDR E)) (MINUSP (CADDR E))) (GO X)))  225
    (PRIN PLUSS)                                                  226
    (PRIN BLANK)                                                  227
  X (PRE2IN (CADDR E)))))                                         228

(XMINUS (LAMBDA (E)                                               229
  (PROG ()                                                        230
    (PRIN DASH)                                                   231
    (PRIN BLANK)                                                  232
    (PRE2IN (CADR E)))))                                          233
```

```
(XTIMES (LAMBDA (E)                                            234
  (PROG (X)                                                    235
    (SETQ X (QUOTE (PLUS MINUS)))                              236
    (COND ((ATOM (CADR E)) (PRIN (CADR E)))                    237
          ((MEMBER (CAADR E) X) (WRAP (CADR E)))               238
          (T (PRE2IN (CADR E))))                               239
    (COND ((ATOM (CADDR E)) (PRIN (CADDR E)))                  240
          ((MEMBER (CAADDR E) X) (WRAP (CADDR E)))             241
          (T (PRE2IN (CADDR E)))))))                           242

(XQUOTIENT (LAMBDA (E)                                         243
  (PROG (X)                                                    244
    (SETQ X (QUOTE (PLUS MINUS)))                              245
    (COND ((ATOM (CADR E)) (PRIN (CADR E)))                    246
          ((MEMBER (CAADR E) X) (WRAP (CADR E)))               247
          (T (PRE2IN (CADR E))))                               248
    (PRIN SLASH)                                               249
    (COND ((ATOM (CADDR E)) (PRIN (CADDR E)))                  250
          ((MEMBER (CAADDR E) X) (WRAP (CADDR E)))             251
          (T (PRE2IN (CADDR E)))))))                           252

(XEXPT (LAMBDA (E)                                             253
  (PROG ()                                                     254
    (COND ((ATOM (CADR E)) (PRIN (CADR E)))                    255
          (T (WRAP (CADR E))))                                 256
    (PRIN UPARROW)                                             257
    (PRIN (CADDR E)))))                                        258

(WRAP (LAMBDA (TERM)                                           259
  (PROG ()                                                     260
    (PRIN LPAR)                                                261
    (PRE2IN TERM)                                              262
    (PRIN RPAR))))                                             263
```

20.7   DIFF

DIFF is the supervisor for the complete program. It controls the evaluation of
the previously discussed functions, and input-output.

MAPCAR is used (line 267) to print the output message

THE DERIVATIVE OF-

whereupon, control is given to the function READER (line 281) to return a list
of all the non-blank characters of the infix *expression* to be differentiated.
To satisfy the demands of READER, the infix *expression* must be terminated by
a comma (line 286). If the *expression* ends with a period, READER returns the
value END (line 285) and DIFF exits to EVALQUOTE with the value FINIS (line 272).
If the *expression* returned by READER can't be translated by IN2PRE, IN2PRE
prints the message

(POORLY FORMED EXPRESSION)

and DIFF tries again (line 273). If the translation is successful, DIFF prints
the message

WITH RESPECT TO-

and READER is called again (line 276) to read the *variable* of differentiation;
it must be a literal atom.

The message

IS-

is printed and DIFF calls DERIV, SIMPLIFY, and PRE2IN in order to perform
differentiation, simplification, and infix translation, respectively (line 278).
Since PRE2IN prints its result directly, DIFF just repeats the loop for another
expression.

Note the use of the $$-artifact to print non-parenthesized output messages.
The free variable DIGITS, noted earlier, is CSET to a list of pairs of literal
atoms and numeric atoms for each *digit*. The function DIGIT uses ASSOC (line 8)
to search this list for equality of the literal atom returned by READCH, and
the CAR of each pair, e.g., $$$0$, $$$1$, etc. When the equality is satisfied,
i.e., ASSOC returns a non-NIL value, the CADR of the pair yields the numeric
value of the literal atom read (line 10).

```
  (DIFF (LAMBDA ()                                                    264
    (PROG (X Y)                                                       265
    A (TERPRI)                                                        266
      (MAPCAR (QUOTE (THE DERIVATIVE $$$OF-$))                        267
              (FUNCTION (LAMBDA (J) (PROG2 (PRIN J) (PRIN BLANK)))))) 268
      (TERPRI)                                                        269
      (TEREAD)                                                        270
      (SETQ X (READER))                                              271
      (COND ((EQUAL X (QUOTE END)) (RETURN (QUOTE FINIS)))            272
            ((NULL (SETQ X (IN2PRE X))) (GO A)))                      273
    B (PRINT (QUOTE $$$ WITH RESPECT TO-$))                           274
      (TEREAD)                                                        275
      (COND ((NOT (ATOM (SETQ Y (CAR (READER))))) (GO B)))            276
      (PRINT (QUOTE $$$IS-$))                                         277
      (PRE2IN (SIMPLIFY (DERIV X Y)))                                 278
      (TERPRI)                                                        279
      (GO A))))                                                       280

  (READER (LAMBDA ()                                                  281
    (PROG (X Y)                                                       282
    A (SETQ X (READCH))                                               283
      (COND ((EQ X BLANK) (GO A))                                     284
            ((EQ X PERIOD) (RETURN (QUOTE END)))                      285
            ((EQ X COMMA) (RETURN (REVERSE Y))))                      286
      (SETQ Y (CONS X Y))                                             287
      (GO A))))                                                       288
```

With the program now completely described, we can examine a few typical examples
of its operation.

```
                    DIFF ( )
                    THE DERIVATIVE OF-
                    Y,
                    WITH RESPECT TO-
                    X,
                    IS-
                    0

                    THE DERIVATIVE OF-
                    X+3,
                    WITH RESPECT TO-
                    X,
                    IS-
                    1

                    THE DERIVATIVE OF-
                    3X↑3,
                    WITH RESPECT TO-
                    X,
                    IS-
                    9 X↑2

                    THE DERIVATIVE OF-
                    3X↑2-2X-4,
                    WITH RESPECT TO-
                    X,
                    IS-
                    6 X -2

                    THE DERIVATIVE OF-
                    3X↑3 + 2X↑2+X+3,
                    WITH RESPECT TO-
                    X,
                    IS-
                    9 X↑2 + 4 X + 1
```

```
                    THE DERIVATIVE OF-
                    3(X↑2 + X) + 2X↑3,
                    WITH RESPECT TO-
                    X,
                    IS-
                    3 (2 X + 1 ) + 6 X↑2

                    THE DERIVATIVE OF-
                    (X+Y)*(X-Y)
                    WITH RESPECT TO-
                    X,
                    IS-
                    X - Y + X + Y
```

Since the input *expression* in this example was not in simplest form, the answer is not in simplified form.

```
                    THE DERIVATIVE OF-
                    B+B)*(A-B),
                    (POORLY FORMED EXPRESSION)

                    THE DERIVATIVE OF-
                    .
                    FINIS
```

APPENDIX A
EXERCISE ANSWERS

CHAPTER 2.

1. Yes
2. No. This is an example of two literal atoms.
3. Yes
4. Yes
5. No. There are no parentheses in an atomic symbol.
6. Yes
7. Yes
8. Yes
9. No. This is a dotted pair.
10. No. First character not a letter. (On some systems this may be an acceptable literal atom because it is obviously not a number.)
11. No. Parentheses missing.
12. No. Parentheses missing.
13. No. Too many dots without proper parentheses.
14. Yes
15. Yes
16.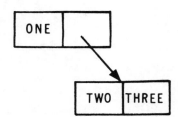

17.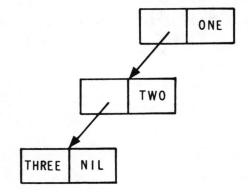

18.

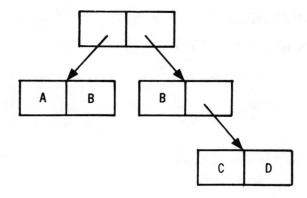

19. (A . (B . ((C . NIL) . (D . NIL))))
20. (((A . B) . (C . D)) . (E . ((F . G) . H)))

CHAPTER 3.

1. (ATOM . NIL)

2. ((LISP . NIL) . NIL)

3. (((MORE . (YET . NIL)) . NIL) . NIL)

4. (HOW . (ABOUT . (THIS . NIL)))

5. (DONT . ((GET . ((FOOLED . NIL) . NIL)) . NIL))

6. (X1)

7. (NIL X1)

8. (KNOW THY SELF)

9. ((BEFORE AND AFTER))

10. (A ((B C)))

11. ((W)) ≡ ((W . NIL) . NIL)

12. (NIL NIL NIL) ≡ (NIL . (NIL . (NIL . NIL)))

13. (W (B) B) ≡ (W . ((B . NIL) . (B . NIL)))

14. (((((NEST)))) ≡ (((((NEST . NIL) . NIL) . NIL) . NIL)

15. (((A) B) (C) D) ≡ (((A . NIL) . (B . NIL)) . ((C . NIL) . (D . NIL)))

CHAPTER 4.

1. Yes

2. Yes (5 E)

3. Yes (E5 . 5)

4. Yes (1.0 . 1Q)

5. Yes Q3 is a literal atom and not 0 X 8^3

6. Yes 4.4

7. No

8. Yes (B . 9.9)

9. No

> Note that the use of blanks to delimit the "CONS dot"
> in 7 and 9 would make these legal S-expressions.

10. Yes (1.23 77Q3 27 2700000 3.21E-8 ALPHA Q . 32)

11. (99.9)

12. (NIL . 99.9)

13. Not a legal S-expression as there are too many dots.

14. (5 5.5 5Q5 5.5 500)

15. ((13.13) (25Q2))

CHAPTER 5.

1. LEFT

2. RIGHT

3. (LEFT . RIGHT)

4. A

5. (A)

6. A

7. (A . B)

8. (SENTENCE IS A LIST)

9. ((ABOUT THIS))

10. ((DOT . PAIR2))

11. (CAR . CDR)

12. NIL ≡ ( )

13. (CDR)

14. (CAR)

15. (A)

16. (75Q . 100)

17. 1

18. (2.0 3.0 . 77Q) ≡ (2.0 . (3.0 . 77Q))

19. ((A . B))

20. ((((ALPHA))))

   The relationship among CONS, CAR, and CDR is that CONS puts together that which CAR and CDR tear apart. More exactly, if the argument to CAR and to CDR is the same S-expression, s, and the two arguments to CONS are the values of the CAR and CDR of this S-expression, then the value of CONS is the original S-expression, i.e., (CONS (CAR s) (CDR s)) = s.

21. CAR CDR CAR = CADAR

22. CAR CAR = CAAR

23. CAR CDR = CADR

24. CDR = CDR

25. CAR CDR CDR = CADDR

26. CAR CDR CDR CDR = CADDDR

27. CAR CAR = CAAR

28. CDR CAR = CDAR

29. CAR CAR CAR CDR = CAAADR

30. CAR CAR CDR = CAADR

31. CAR CDR CAR CDR = CADADR

CHAPTER 6.

	Variable	Binding
1.	X	ATOM
2.	Y	(LIST)
3.	J	(THREE ELEMENT LIST)
4.	K	(THREE ELEMENT LIST)
5.	U	VERY
	V	GOOD
6.	Y	ONE
	X	(THEN . ANOTHER)
7.	A	(A (B . 77Q2))
8.	VARIABLE	((A B))
9.	J	NIL
10.	empty	empty
11.	U	ALPHA
	V	BETA

	Variable	Binding
12.	U	BETA
	V	ALPHA
13.	U	ALPHA
	V	BETA
14.	V	ALPHA
	U	BETA
15.	FIRST	(FIRST)
	SECOND	SECOND

CHAPTER 7.

1. ATOM
2. (LIST)
3. THREE
4. (ELEMENT LIST)
5. (VERY . GOOD)
6. (ONE THEN . ANOTHER) ≡ (ONE . (THEN . ANOTHER))
7. B
8. (B)
9. 3.14159
10. 3.14159
11. ALPHA
12. BETA
13. BETA
14. ALPHA
15. FIRST

CHAPTER 8.

1. 43
2. LIST
3. NIL
4. 43
5. NUMBER
6. Y
7. (((LIST)))

8. B

9. 123Q3

10. (A . B)

11. (LAMBDA (J) (CAR (CDR (CDR J)))) ((1 2 3 4)) = 3

12. (LAMBDA (X) (CAR (CAR X))) (((A B C) D)) = A

13. (LAMBDA (Y) (CAR (CDR Y))) (((A B C) D)) = D

14. (LAMBDA (Z) (CDR (CAR Z))) (((A B C) D)) = (B C)

15. (LAMBDA (VARIABLE) (CAR (CDR (CAR VARIABLE)))) (((A B C) D)) = B

16. (A C)

17. (A C)

18. (A)

19. (C)

20. ((B A) (D C))

CHAPTER 9.

1. X

2. J

3. (AN S EXPRESSION)

4. A

5. (J)

6. (QUOTE . EXPR)

7. CAR ((A . BETA)) = A

8. (NOW IS THE TIME FOR ALL GOOD MEN TO COME TO THE AID OF THE PARTY)

9. (A . B)

10. (LAMBDA (X) X)

11. (ONE TWO THREE)

12. (ONE TWO THREE)

13. (NIL F NIL F NIL F)

14. (F F F F F F)

15. ((NIL F F) (T T T) (NIL NIL NIL) (123 123 123))

16. X

17. J

18. (AN S EXPRESSION)

19. A

20. (J)

21. ABLE

22. (ABLE QUOTE ABLE)

23. EVAL ((CAR (QUOTE (ABLE)))) = ABLE

24. (CONS A B)

25. EVAL ((CDR (QUOTE (A B)))) = (B)

CHAPTER 10.

1. DEFINE (((FIRST (LAMBDA (X) (CAR X)))))
       FIRST ((A B C D E)) = A

2-4. DEFINE ((
           (SECOND (LAMBDA (Y) (CADR Y)))
           (THIRD (LAMBDA (Z) (CAR (CDDR Z))))
           (CADDDDR (LAMBDA (J) (CAR (CDDDDR J))))
        ))
     SECOND ((A B C D E)) = B
     THIRD ((A B C D E)) = C
     CADDDDR ((A B C D E)) = E

5. DEFINE (((REVDOT (LAMBDA (J) (CONS (CDR J) (CAR J))))))
   REVDOT ((A . B)) = (B . A)
   REVDOT (((A) . (B))) = ((B) . (A)) = ((B) A)
   REVDOT ((((FIRST)) . (LAST))) = ((LAST) . ((FIRST))) = ((LAST) (FIRST))

CHAPTER 11.

1. TRUE

2. 1

3. Undefined, as there is no non-NIL conditional clause.

4. (T)

5. NOP

6. DEFINE (((OR2 (LAMBDA (X Y) (COND (X T) (Y T) (T NIL))))))

7. DEFINE (((XOR2 (LAMBDA (X Y)
       (COND (X (COND (Y NIL) (T T))) (Y T) (T NIL))))))

8. DEFINE (((AND2 (LAMBDA (X Y)
       (COND (X (COND (Y T) (T NIL))) (T NIL))))))

9. (SELECT T $(p_1\ e_1)$ $(p_2\ e_2)$ ... $(p_n\ e_n)$ (error))

10. (COND ((EQUAL p p_1) e_1) ((EQUAL p p_2) e_2) ...
         ((EQUAL p p_n) e_n) (T e))

CHAPTER 12.

1. (T F T F)
2. T
3. T
4. NIL
5. T
6. NIL
7. T
8. NIL
9. T
10. NIL
11. NIL
12. T
13. T
14. T
15. NIL, since HEAR is not a top-level member of list (NOW (HEAR THIS)).
        Rather, HEAR is a member of the sublist (HEAR THIS), and MEMBER
        tests only for elements at the top level of a list.
16. T
17. DEFINE (((EQUIV (LAMBDA (X Y) (EQ X Y)))))
18. DEFINE (((IMPLIES (LAMBDA (X Y) (OR (EQ X Y) Y)))))
19. This program can be easily written with conditionals and recursion.
    However, since the student has not learned these techniques, the following
    expression is required (see exercise 19 of Chapter 14 for recursive solution):

    DEFINE ((
    (INSEQ (LAMBDA (J)
      ((LAMBDA (V W X Y Z) (AND
        (AND (NUMBERP V) (NUMBERP W) (NUMBERP X) (NUMBERP Y) (NUMBERP Z))
        (OR (AND (LESSP V W) (LESSP W X) (LESSP X Y) (LESSP Y Z))
            (AND (GREATERP V W) (GREATERP W X) (GREATERP X Y) (GREATERP Y Z)))))
            (CAR J) (CADR J) (CADDR J) (CADDDR J) (CAR (CDDDDR J)))))
    ))

Note that the use of nested lambda expressions permits us to bind V to the first list element, W to the second, X to the third, etc. This practice creates temporary storage for these partial results and simplifies the total expression as well as reduces the total computation, since we need compute these repeatedly used arguments only once.

20. DEFINE (((EQN (LAMBDA (X Y) (OR (EQ X Y)

                                      (AND (NUMBERP X)

                                      (NUMBERP Y)

                                      (ZEROP (DIFFERENCE X Y))))))))

CHAPTER 13.

1. 55

2. 95.85841

3. 1024

4. 32768

5. 0.0

6. 0

7. 10.000000001

8. 9.999999999

9. 18

10. 18.333333333

11. 1 i.e., a number-theoretic remainder for fixed-point arguments.

12. 9.3132257461E-10 i.e., floating-point residue for floating-point arguments.

13. (18 1)

14. (18.333333333 9.3132257461E-10)

15. (18 1)

16. 123

17. -123

18. 0

19. 0

20. 5.0

21. 0.333333333

22. 0

23. 1.2345678900E+8

24. 3.14159

25. 77777Q

26. 717375Q

27. 765435Q

28. 715335Q

29. 12345Q

30. 204Q1

31. 16Q1

32. 34Q

33. DEFINE (((TRIPLE (LAMBDA (X) (PLUS X X X)))))

34. DEFINE (((CUBE (LAMBDA (X) (TIMES X X X)))))

35. DEFINE (((SIMPLEINTEREST (LAMBDA (PRINCIPAL RATE YEARS)

    (TIMES PRINCIPAL (ADD1 (TIMES YEARS RATE)))))))

36. DEFINE (((ANNUALCOMPOUND (LAMBDA (P R Y)

    (TIMES P (EXPT (ADD1 R) Y))))))

37. DEFINE (((TIMECOMPOUND (LAMBDA (P R Y T)

    (TIMES P (EXPT (ADD1 (QUOTIENT R T)) (TIMES T Y)))))))

38. DEFINE (((TWOBY (LAMBDA (A11 A12 A21 A22)

    (DIFFERENCE (TIMES A11 A22) (TIMES A12 A21))))))

39. DEFINE (((THREEBY (LAMBDA (A11 A12 A13 A21 A22 A23 A31 A32 A33)

    (PLUS (TIMES A11 (TWOBY A22 A23 A32 A33))

        (MINUS (TIMES A12 (TWOBY A21 A23 A31 A33)))

    (TIMES A13 (TWOBY A21 A22 A31 A32)))))))

40. DEFINE (((SOLVE (LAMBDA (A11 A12 A13 A21 A22 A23 A31 A32 A33 C1 C2 C3)

    ((LAMBDA (U1 U2 U3 D) (LIST (CONS (QUOTE U1) (QUOTIENT U1 D))

                                (CONS (QUOTE U2) (QUOTIENT U2 D))

                                (CONS (QUOTE U3) (QUOTIENT U3 D))))

    (THREEBY C1 A12 A13 C2 A22 A23 C3 A32 A33)

    (THREEBY A11 C1 A13 A21 C2 A23 A31 C3 A33)

    (THREEBY A11 A12 C1 A21 A22 C2 A31 A32 C3)

    (THREEBY A11 A12 A13 A21 A22 A23 A31 A32 A33))))))

    1. SOLVE (2 1 -2 1 1 1 -1 -2 3 -6 2 12) = ((U1 . 1) (U2 . -2) (U3 . 3))

    2. SOLVE (2 1 -2 2 1 3 -1 -2 3 5 6 12) = (U1 . 7) (U2 . -9) (U3 . 0))

    3. SOLVE (15 15 15 7 1 -100 -50 1 1 15 -100 -16) = ((U1 . 0) (U2 . 0) (U3 . 1))

    4. SOLVE (1 2 -2 1 1 1 -2 -1 3 -12 6 2) = ((U1 . 8) (U2 . -6) (U3 . 4))

    5. SOLVE (-2 2 1 1 1 1 3 -1 -2 -24 49 9) = ((U1 . 22) (U2 . -5) (U3 . 32))

CHAPTER 14.

1. A

    B

    Z

    NIL

    NIL

2. X

    E

    NO

    L

3. DEFINE (((TWIST (LAMBDA (S) (COND ((ATOM S) S)

                              (T (CONS (TWIST (CDR S))

                                    (TWIST (CAR S)))))))))

    A

    (B . A)

    (C . (B . A)) = (C B . A)

    (((NIL . C) . B) . A)

    (NIL . (B . A)) = (NIL B . A)

4. DEFINE (((SUM (LAMBDA (X Y) (COND ((ZEROP Y) X) (T (SUM (ADD1 X) (SUB1 Y)))))))))

    ARGS OF SUM

      1

      2

    ARGS OF SUM

      2

      1

    ARGS OF SUM

      3

      0

    VALUE OF SUM

      3

    VALUE OF SUM

      3

    VALUE OF SUM

      3

```
5.  DEFINE (( (PROD (LAMBDA (X Y) (COND ((ZEROP Y) 0)
                                   (T (SUM X (PROD X (SUB1 Y))))))) ))

6.  DEFINE (( (REMXY (LAMBDA (X Y) (COND ((LESSP X Y) X)
                                    ((EQUAL X Y) 0)
                                    (T (REMXY (DIFFERENCE X Y) Y))))) ))

7.  DEFINE (( (COUNT (LAMBDA (E)
        (COND ((NULL E) 0) ((ATOM E) 1)
              (T (PLUS (COUNT (CAR E)) (COUNT (CDR E))))))) ))

8.  DEFINE (( (FIBB (LAMBDA (N)
        (COND ((ONEP N) 1) ((EQUAL 2 N) 1)
              (T (PLUS (FIBB (SUB1 N)) (FIBB (DIFFERENCE N 2))))))) ))

9.  DEFINE (( (GCD (LAMBDA (X Y) (COND ((GREATERP X Y) (GCD Y X))
                                  ((ZEROP (REMAINDER Y X)) X)
                                  (T (GCD X (REMAINDER Y X)))))) ))

10. DEFINE (( (AMONG (LAMBDA (A L) (COND ((NULL L) NIL)
                                    ((EQ A (CAR L)) T)
                                    (T (AMONG A (CDR L)))))) ))

11. DEFINE (( (INSIDE (LAMBDA (A E) (COND ((ATOM E) (EQ A E))
                                     ((INSIDE A (CAR E)) T)
                                     (T (INSIDE A (CDR E)))))) ))

12. DEFINE (( (COPYN (LAMBDA (X N) (COND ((ZEROP N) NIL)
                                    (T (CONS X (COPYN X (SUB1 N))))))) ))

13. DEFINE (( (LENGTHS (LAMBDA (L) (COND ((NULL L) 0)
                                    (T (ADD1 (LENGTHS (CDR L))))))) ))

14. DEFINE (( (UNIONS (LAMBDA (X Y) (COND ((NULL X) Y)
                                     ((MEMBER (CAR X) Y) (UNIONS (CDR X) Y))
                                     (T (CONS (CAR X) (UNIONS (CDR X) Y)))))) ))

15. DEFINE (( (INTERSECT (LAMBDA (X Y) (COND ((NULL X) NIL)
                                        ((MEMBER (CAR X) Y) (CONS (CAR X)
                                             (INTERSECT (CDR X) Y)))
                                        (T (INTERSECT (CDR X) Y))))) ))

16. DEFINE (( (REVERSAL (LAMBDA (L) (COND ((NULL L) NIL)
                                     (T (APPEND (REVERSAL (CDR L))
                                              (LIST (CAR L))))))) ))
```

```
17.  DEFINE (( (PAIRS (LAMBDA (L1 L2) (COND ((NULL L1) NIL)
                                     (T (CONS (CONS (CAR L1) (CAR L2))
                                     (PAIRS (CDR L1) (CAR L2)))))))) ))

18.  DEFINE (( (DELETE (LAMBDA (A L) (COND ((NULL L) NIL)
                                     ((EQ A (CAR L)) (DELETE A (CDR L)))
                                     (T (CONS (CAR L) (DELETE A (CDR L))))))) ))

19.  DEFINE ((
           (INSEQ (LAMBDA (L) (OR (INSEQA L) (INSEQA (REVERSE L)))))
           (INSEQA (LAMBDA (L) (COND ((NULL L) T)
                                ((NULL (CDR L)) T)
                                ((NOT (NUMBERP (CAR L))) NIL)
                                ((NOT (NUMBERP (CADR L))) NIL)
                                ((LESSP (CAR L) (CADR L)) (INSEQA (CDR L)))
                                (T NIL))))
     ))

20.  DEFINE (( (REPLACE (LAMBDA (A B X) (COND ((ATOM X) (COND ((EQUAL B X) A) (T X)))
                                     (T (CONS (REPLACE A B (CAR X))
                                     (REPLACE A B (CDR X))))))) ))
```

CHAPTER 15.

```
1.  DEFINE (( (NEGCNT (LAMBDA (L) (PROG (X)
            (SETQ X 0)
      TAG1  (COND ((NULL L) (RETURN X))
            ((MINUSP (CAR L)) (SETQ X (ADD1 X))))
            (SETQ L (CDR L))
            (GO TAG1)))) ))

2.  DEFINE (( (CURVE (LAMBDA (A B C) (PROG (X)
            (SETQ X (PLUS (TIMES B B) (TIMES -4 A C)))
            (COND ((ZEROP X) (RETURN (QUOTE PARABOLA)))
                  ((LESSP X 0) (RETURN (QUOTE ELLIPSE))))
            (RETURN (QUOTE HYPERBOLA))))) ))

3.  DEFINE (( (LENGTHS (LAMBDA (M) (PROG (X)
            (SETQ X 0)
      LOC1  (COND ((NULL M) (RETURN X)))
            (SETQ X (ADD1 X))
```

```
                    (SETQ M (CDR M))
                    (GO LOC1)))) ))
  4.  DEFINE (( (LAST (LAMBDA (L) (PROG (U)
          T1   (COND ((NULL L) (RETURN U)))
               (SETQ U (CAR L))
               (SETQ L (CDR L))
               (GO T1)))) ))
5-7.  DEFINE ((
               (REVERSAL (LAMBDA (L) (PROG (Y)
          T2   (COND ((NULL L) (RETURN Y)))
               (SETQ Y (CONS (CAR L) Y))
               (SETQ L (CDR L))
               (GO T2))))
               (PAIRS (LAMBDA (L1 L2) (PROG (X)
          T3   (COND ((NULL L1) (RETURN (REVERSE X))))
               (SETQ X (CONS (CONS (CAR L1) (CAR L2)) X))
               (SETQ L1 (CDR L1))
               (SETQ L2 (CDR L2))
               (GO T3))))
               (DELETE (LAMBDA (A L) (PROG (Z)
          T4   (COND ((NULL L) (RETURN (REVERSE Z)))
                    ((EQ A (CAR L)) (GO T5)))
               (SETQ Z (CONS (CAR L) Z))
          T5   (SETQ L (CDR L))
               (GO T4))))
            ))
  8.  DEFINE (( (PERMUT (LAMBDA (N R)
               (QUOTIENT (FACTORIAL N) (FACTORIAL (DIFFERENCE N R))))) ))
      DEFINE (( (PERMUT (LAMBDA (N R) (PROG ( )
               (RETURN (QUOTIENT (FACTORIAL N) (FACTORIAL (DIFFERENCE N R)))))))) ))
  9.  DEFINE (( (COMBIN (LAMBDA (N R)
               (QUOTIENT (FACTORIAL N) (TIMES (FACTORIAL R)
                                       (FACTORIAL (DIFFERENCE N R)))))) ))
```

```
DEFINE ((  (COMBIN (LAMBDA (N R) (PROG ( )
              (RETURN (QUOTIENT (FACTORIAL N)
                         (TIMES (FACTORIAL R)
                            (FACTORIAL (DIFFERENCE N R))) ))))) ))
```

10.
```
DEFINE ((  (PASCAL (LAMBDA (N) (PROG (X R LINE)
              (SETQ X 0)
OUTLOOP     (SETQ R 0)
              (COND ((LESSP N X) (RETURN NIL)))
  INLOOP    (COND ((LESSP X R) (GO BUMPX)))
              (SETQ LINE (CONS (COMBIN X R) LINE))
              (SETQ R (ADD1 R))
              (GO INLOOP)
  BUMPX     (PRINT LINE)
              (SETQ LINE NIL)
              (SETQ X (ADD1 X))
              (GO OUTLOOP)))) ))
```

```
PASCAL(15)
 (1)
 (1 1)
 (1 2 1)
 (1 3 3 1)
 (1 4 6 4 1)
 (1 5 10 10 5 1)
 (1 6 15 20 15 6 1)
 (1 7 21 35 35 21 7 1)
 (1 8 28 56 70 56 28 8 1)
 (1 9 36 84 126 126 84 36 9 1)
 (1 10 45 120 210 252 210 120 45 10 1)
 (1 11 55 165 330 462 462 330 165 55 11 1)
 (1 12 66 220 495 792 924 792 495 220 66 12 1)
 (1 13 78 286 715 1287 1716 1716 1287 715 286 78 13 1)
 (1 14 91 364 1001 2002 3003 3432 3003 2002 1001 364 91 14 1)
 (1 15 105 455 1365 3003 5005 6435 6435 5005 3003 1365 455 105 15 1)
 NIL
```

PASCAL (16) is the largest triangle possible with this definition since 16! is maximum fixed-point accuracy of a 48-bit machine.

CHAPTER 16.

There are no exercises for this chapter.

CHAPTER 17.

1. (LIST)
   (LIST)

2. blank line
   NIL
   blank line
   NIL

3. ATOM1 ATOM2
   NIL

4. (NOW HEAR THIS)

5. ((INPUT) ANYTHING)

6. For R=5 , 31.4159
   For R=50 , 314.159
   For R=10 , 62.8318
   For END , END

7. (( ) . / = $ * NOW HEAR THIS -533.17)

8. (B C)

9. 1. % This expression binds the literal atom $$*%* to the name PERCENT.
      The $$-artifact is the only way to enter illegal read characters.
   2. %
   3. PERCENT

10. A

11. 1. A
    2. (B C)
    3. (A . B)
    4. 3.14159
    5. 3.14159

12. 1. (A)
    2. (A . B)

```
3.   3.14159
4.   (3.14159)
5.   X       SQUARE
     0        0
     1        1
     2        4
     3        9
     4       16
     5       25
     6       36
     7       49
     8       64
     9       81
     END
```

13.   DEFINE ((

```
(SUP4 (LAMBDA ( ) (PROG (S1 S2 ARGS)
A    (TEREAD) (SETQ ARGS NIL)
     (SETQ S2 (READ))
     (SETQ S1 (READ))
B    (COND ((NULL S2) (GO C)))
     (SETQ ARGS (CONS (LIST (QUOTE QUOTE) (CAR S2)) ARGS))
     (SETQ S2 (CDR S2))
     (GO B)
C    (PRINT (EVAL (CONS S1 (REVERSE ARGS))))
     (GO A) )))
          ))
```

1.   A
2.   (B C)
3.   NIL
4.   10
5.   3.14159
6.   3.14159

```
14.  DEFINE ((
     (SUP5 (LAMBDA ( ) (PROG (X Y Z)
     A   (TEREAD) (SETQ Z NIL)
         (SETQ X (READ))
         (SETQ Y (READ))
         (PRIN X) (PRIN Y) (TERPRI)
         (COND ((EQ (QUOTE NO) (READ)) (GO A)))
         (PRIN X) (PRIN Y) (PRIN BLANK) (PRIN1 EQSIGN) (PRIN BLANK)
     B   (COND ((NULL Y) (GO C)))
         (SETQ Z (CONS (LIST (QUOTE QUOTE) (CAR Y)) Z))
         (SETQ Y (CDR Y))
         (GO B)
     C   (PRIN (EVAL (CONS X (REVERSE Z))))
         (TERPRI)
         (GO A)))) ))
15.  DEFINE (( (PI (LAMBDA (X) (PROG (HI)
                   (PRINT (QUOTE (ENTER MAX X)))
                   (SETQ HI (READ))
                   (SETQ X (TIMES X 1.0))
                   (PRINT (QUOTE $$$

     X          XSQUARE           SQRTX           RECIPX           FACTORIALX
$))
     TAG1          (COND ((LESSP HI X) (RETURN (QUOTE $$$LIMIT REACHED$))))
                   (PRIN1 X)
                   (PRIN $$$          $)
                   (PRIN1 (TIMES X X))
                   (PRIN $$$          $)
                   (PRIN1 (SQRT X))
                   (PRIN $$$   $)
                   (PRIN1 (QUOTIENT 1.0 X))
                   (PRIN $$$   $)
                   (PRIN1 (FACTORIAL X))
                   (TERPRI)
                   (SETQ X (ADD1 X))
                   (GO TAG1)))) ))
```

CHAPTER 18.

1. (TRY THIS SIMPLE CASE FIRST)
    (THIS SIMPLE CASE FIRST)
    (SIMPLE CASE FIRST)
    (CASE FIRST)
    (FIRST)
    NIL
2. NOW
    THIS
    ONE
    NIL
3. AND
    LASTLY
    THIS
    ONE
    (AND LASTLY THIS ONE)
4. ((ONE 2 3 ONE 4 ONE 5) (2 3 ONE 4 ONE 5) (3 ONE 4 ONE 5) (ONE 4 ONE 5)
    (4 ONE 5) (ONE 5) (5))
5. ((1 2 3 4) (2 3 4) (3 4) (4))
6. ((A . A) (B . B) (C . C) (D . D) (E . E))
7. ((A . X) (B . X) (C . X) (D . X) (E . X))
8. ((A . Z) (B . Z) (C . Z) (D . Z) (E . Z))
    ((A 1 2 3 4 5) (B 1 2 3 4 5) (C 1 2 3 4 5) (D 1 2 3 4 5) (E 1 2 3 4 5))
9. DEFINE ((
        (MAPCAR2 (LAMBDA (X Y FN)
            (COND ((NULL X) NIL)
                (T (CONS (FN (CAR X) (CAR Y)) (MAPCAR2 (CDR X) (CDR Y) FN))))))))
10. DEFINE ((
        (TYPE (LAMBDA (J) (MAPCAR J (FUNCTION
            (LAMBDA (K) (COND ((NUMBERP K) (RETURN (COND ((FIXP K) (QUOTE FIX))
                                                    (T (QUOTE FLT)))))
                        ((ATOM K) (QUOTE ATOM))
                        ((EQ (ATOM (CAR K)) (ATOM (CDR K))) (QUOTE DOTPAIR))
                        (T (QUOTE LIST))))))))))

CHAPTER 19.

1. ((CAT) (DOG) (FOX) 1 2 3.0)

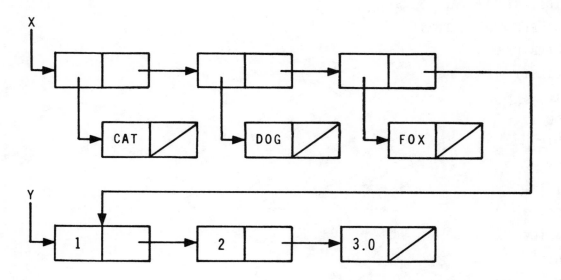

2. (1 (2 3.0))

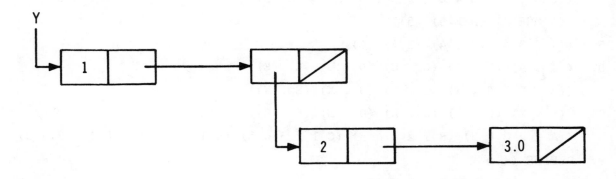

3. (NCONC (LAMBDA (X Y) (PROG (M)

      (COND ((NULL X) (RETURN Y)))

      (SETQ M X)

   A (COND ((NULL (CDR M)) (GO B)))

      (SETQ M (CDR M))

      (GO A)

   B (RPLACD M Y)

      (RETURN X))))

```
4.    (REVLIST (LAMBDA (L) (PROG (C P)
         A (SETQ C L)
           (COND ((NULL L) (RETURN P)))
           (SETQ L (CDR L))
           (RPLACD C P)
           (SETQ P C)
           (GO A) )))
5.    (BLAM (LAMBDA (L) (PROG (M)
           (SETQ M L)
         A (COND ((NULL M) (RETURN L)))
           (RPLACA M (CDR M))
           (SETQ M (CDR M))
           (GO A) )))
6.    (SUITS (LAMBDA (PLAYER) (PROG (S H D C X)
           (SETQ X (GET PLAYER (QUOTE HAND)))
         A (COND ((NULL X) (GO B)))
           (SELECT (GET (CAR X) (QUOTE SUIT))
                   ((QUOTE SPADE) (SETQ S (CONS (CAR X) S)))
                   ((QUOTE HEART) (SETQ H (CONS (CAR X) H)))
                   ((QUOTE DIAMOND) (SETQ D (CONS (CAR X) D)))
                   (SETQ C (CONS (CAR X) C)))
           (SETQ X (CDR X))
           (GO A)
         B (PUT PLAYER (QUOTE SPADES) S)
           (PUT PLAYER (QUOTE HEARTS) H)
           (PUT PLAYER (QUOTE DIAMONDS) D)
           (PUT PLAYER (QUOTE CLUBS) C)
           (RETURN PLAYER) )))
7.    (LONGSUIT (LAMBDA (PLAYER) (PROG (S H D C HI1 HI2)
         (SETQ S (LENGTH (GET PLAYER (QUOTE SPADES))))
         (SETQ H (LENGTH (GET PLAYER (QUOTE HEARTS))))
         (SETQ D (LENGTH (GET PLAYER (QUOTE DIAMONDS))))
         (SETQ C (LENGTH (GET PLAYER (QUOTE CLUBS))))
```

```
            (COND ((GREATERP H S) (SETQ HI1 (CONS (QUOTE HEARTS) H)))
                  (T (SETQ HI1 (CONS (QUOTE SPADES) S))))
            (COND ((GREATERP C D) (SETQ HI2 (CONS (QUOTE CLUBS) C)))
                  (T (SETQ HI2 (CONS (QUOTE DIAMONDS) D))))
            (COND ((GREATERP (CDR HI2) (CDR HI1)) (RETURN HI2))
                  (T (RETURN HI1))) )))
8.  (POINTS (LAMBDA (PLAYER)
          (PLUS (POINT1 PLAYER (QUOTE SPADES))
                (POINT1 PLAYER (QUOTE HEARTS))
                (POINT1 PLAYER (QUOTE DIAMONDS))
                (POINT1 PLAYER (QUOTE CLUBS)))))
    (POINT1 (LAMBDA (P S) (PROG (SUM LN VALUE X)
       (SETQ SUM 0)
       (SETQ X (GET P S))
       (SETQ LN (LENGTH X))
       (COND ((ZEROP LN) (RETURN 3)))
A      (COND ((NULL X) (RETURN SUM)))
       (SETQ VALUE (GET (CAR X) (QUOTE RANK)))
       (SETQ SUM (PLUS SUM
            (COND ((LESSP VALUE 11) 0)
                  ((EQUAL VALUE 14) 4)
                  ((AND (EQUAL VALUE 13)
                        (GREATERP LN 1)) 3)
                  ((AND (EQUAL VALUE 12)
                        (GREATERP LN 2)) 2)
                  ((AND (EQUAL VALUE 11)
                        (GREATERP LN 3)) 1)
                  ((ONEP LN) 2)
                  (T 0))))
      (SETQ X (CDR X))
      (GO A) )))
9.  (STOPPERS (LAMBDA (PLAYER) (AND (STOP PLAYER (QUOTE SPADES))
                                    (STOP PLAYER (QUOTE HEARTS))
                                    (STOP PLAYER (QUOTE DIAMONDS))
                                    (STOP PLAYER (QUOTE CLUBS)))))
```

```
        (STOP (LAMBDA (P S) (PROG (LN VALUE X)
           (SETQ X (GET P S))
           (SETQ LN (LENGTH X))
           (COND ((ZEROP LN) (RETURN NIL)))
    A     (COND ((NULL X) (RETURN NIL)))
           (SETQ VALUE (GET (CAR X) (QUOTE RANK)))
        (COND ((OR (EQUAL VALUE 14)
                   (AND (EQUAL VALUE 13)
                        (GREATERP LN 1))
                   (AND (EQUAL VALUE 12)
                        (GREATERP LN 2))) (RETURN T)))
        (SETQ X (CDR X))
        (GO A) )))
10.  (BALANCED (LAMBDA (PLAYER)
           (LESSP 2 (MIN (LENGTH (GET PLAYER (QUOTE SPADES)))
                         (LENGTH (GET PLAYER (QUOTE HEARTS)))
                         (LENGTH (GET PLAYER (QUOTE DIAMONDS)))
                         (LENGTH (GET PLAYER (QUOTE CLUBS))) ))))
     (OPENBID (LAMBDA (PLAYER) (PROG (PT LS ST BAL)
        (SUITS PLAYER)
        (SETQ PT (POINTS PLAYER))
        (SETQ LS (LONGSUIT PLAYER))
        (SETQ ST (STOPPERS PLAYER))
        (SETQ BAL (BALANCED PLAYER))
        (COND ((LESSP PT 13) (GO PASS))
              ((LESSP PT 20) (GO ONEBID))
              ((AND ST BAL) (RETURN (QUOTE (2 NO TRUMP))))
              (T (RETURN (LIST 2 (CAR LS)))))
     PASS (COND ((AND (GREATERP (CDR LS) 6)
                      (GREATERP PT 6))
                 (RETURN (LIST 3 (CAR LS))))
                (T (RETURN (QUOTE PASS))))
     ONEBID (COND ((AND ST BAL (GREATERP PT 15)) (RETURN (QUOTE (1 NO TRUMP))))
                  (T (RETURN (LIST 1 (CAR LS))))) )))
```

```
11.   MACRO (( (PROD (LAMBDA (J) (*EXPAND J (QUOTE *TIMES)))) ))
12.   MACRO ((
      (MAXIMUM (LAMBDA (J) (*EXPAND J (QUOTE *MAX))))
      (MINIMUM (LAMBDA (J) (*EXPAND J (QUOTE *MIN))))
            ))
13.   MACRO (( (FLAMBDA (LAMBDA (J)
                  (LIST (QUOTE FUNCTION)
                      (CONS (QUOTE LAMBDA) (CDR J)))))  ))
14.   MACRO ((
      (LIST2 (LAMBDA (J) (*EXPAND J (QUOTE CONS))))
      (LIST1 (LAMBDA (J) (APPEND (CONS (QUOTE LIST2)
                                       (CDR J))
                                 (QUOTE (NIL)))))
            ))
```

We note here that given a form

$$(\text{LIST1 } x_1 \ x_2 \ x_3) \qquad [1]$$

the macro LIST2 expands form [1] to

$$(\text{LIST2 } x_1 \ x_2 \ x_3 \ \text{NIL}) \qquad [2]$$

and with repeated application to

$$(\text{CONS } x_1 \ (\text{CONS } x_2 \ (\text{CONS } x_3 \ \text{NIL})))$$

Thus the sole purpose of macro LIST1 is to insert NIL as the last argument of the form. If we used the macro definition for LIST2 only, we would get a value of

$$(x_1 \ x_2 \ . \ x_3)$$

rather than

$$(x_1 \ x_2 \ x_3)$$

which is the list we desire.

A more practical solution is to redefine *EXPAND as say *EXPANDS.

```
DEFINE ((
  (*EXPANDS (LAMBDA (FORM FN)
     (COND ((NULL (CDDR FORM))
              (CONS FN (CONS (CADR FORM) (QUOTE (NIL)))))
            (T (CONS FN
                     (CONS (CADR FORM)
                     (CONS (CONS (CAR FORM) (CDDR FORM)) NIL))))))))  ))
```

Then define LIST1 as

```
MACRO ((
  (LIST1 (LAMBDA (J) (*EXPANDS J (QUOTE CONS))))  ))
```

In this approach the form

$$(LIST1\ x_1\ x_2\ x_3)$$

becomes

$$(CONS\ x_1\ (LIST1\ x_2\ x_3))$$

and with repeated application

$$(CONS\ x_1\ (CONS\ x_2\ (LIST1\ x_3)))$$

Here's the difference. *EXPAND would return x_3 as the last term, but *EXPANDS returns (CONS x_3 NIL) and we achieve the same result as above much more efficiently.

15.
```
DEFINE ((
    (PRINTQ1 (LAMBDA (J) (PROG ( )
  T1 (COND ((NULL J) (RETURN (TERPRI))))
     (PRIN (CAR J)) (PRIN BLANK)
     (SETQ J (CDR J))
     (GO T1)))) ))
```

```
     MACRO ((
        (PRINTQ (LAMBDA (J) (LIST (QUOTE PRINTQ1)
                                  (LIST (QUOTE QUOTE)
                                         (CDR J))))) ))
```

The form

```
              (PRINTQ NOW HEAR THIS)
```

after the macro PRINTQ has been executed, will be replaced by the form

```
              (PRINTQ1 (QUOTE (NOW HEAR THIS)))
```

The function PRINTQ1 enters each element of the list into the print line with PRIN, and executes a final TERPRI when the list is empty.

16. MACRO (((PROGN (LAMBDA (J) (*EXPAND J (QUOTE PROG2))))))

APPENDIX B
GLOSSARY

<u>a-list</u>

A synonym for association list.

<u>association list</u>

A list of dotted pairs used by interpretive LISP systems to pair bound
variables with their values. It is of the form

$$((u_1 \cdot v_1) \ (u_2 \cdot v_2) \ \ldots \ (u_n \cdot v_n))$$

<u>atom</u>

A synonym for atomic symbol.

<u>atomic symbol</u>

The elementary form of an S-expression. There are literal atoms and
numeric atoms. A literal atom consists of a string of capital letters
and decimal digits of indefinite length that begins with a letter; e.g.,
A, BOY22, Z1Z2. Numeric atoms are real, integer, or octal numbers distinguished by their syntax. (c.f. Chapter 4)

<u>binding</u>

The association of a variable with a value within some expression context.
There may be multiple bindings for a variable during its lifetime as it is
used in multiple contexts; however, there is only one binding current at
a time. Lambda and program expressions are the principal ways to create
bindings. (See zero-level bindings)

<u>bound variables</u>

A variable named in the list of variables following LAMBDA or PROG in
lambda or program expressions is bound within the scope of that expression.
During evaluation of these expressions, the value of the variable is the
value of the corresponding argument in the function call. For example,
for (LAMBDA (J K) *body*) (1 2), J has value 1 and K has value 2 at any of
their occurrences in the *body*.

character object

A literal atom, the value of which prints as a special character. For example,

CSET (LARROW $$*←*)

creates the character object LARROW, the value of which prints as "←".

clause

A predicate expression and its corresponding form in a conditional expression.

common variable

Variables used for communication between compiled and interpreted expressions for LISP systems having both a compiler and an interpreter.

composed form

The concatenation of forms such that the value of one form is used as the argument for another form. This is written in a nested format, e.g.,

(CONS (CAR X) (CDR X))

conditional expression

An expression containing a list of clauses. The value of the conditional expression is the value of the form corresponding to the first (leftmost) predicate expression that evaluates to non-NIL. Evaluation proceeds left to right only as far as the first non-NIL expression. No form is evaluated if its predicate expression is NIL.

constant

A variable, the value of which never changes during computation, or a quoted expression. The following are examples of constants:

(QUOTE (A B C))
3.14159
T

context

The bindings for variables during a particular computation. For recursive evaluation of a function or an expression, the context at any time is the current state of its variables. Variables used free in an expression are said to be outside the scope of that expression as the expression does not control the bindings of the free variables.

dot notation

The fundamental notation of LISP for representing non-atomic S-expressions. Dot notation contains left parentheses, right parentheses, atoms, and dots. A non-atomic S-expression is always a dotted pair of S-expressions of the form

$$(s_1 \cdot s_2)$$

where s_1 and s_2 are any S-expressions.

dotted pair

A non-atomic S-expression. The value of the expression

$$CONS \ (s_1 \ s_2) = (s_1 \cdot s_2)$$

where s_1 and s_2 are arbitrary S-expressions.

doublet

A pair of S-expressions for EVALQUOTE, the top-level system supervisor. The first S-expression is a function name or a functional expression. The second S-expression is a list of arguments.

dummy variable

If the systematic substitution of a literal atom for one used as a variable in an expression does not change the meaning (i.e., the value returned) of the expression, the variable is a dummy variable. All lambda and program variables are dummy variables.

element

The top-level constituents of a list. These constituents may be atomic or non-atomic. If they are lists, they may themselves have elements. Thus,

( )	has no elements
(A)	has one element
(A (B))	has two elements, one of which is a list of one element.

empty list

A list having no elements. This list is also equivalent to the literal
atom, NIL.

expression

A synonym for S-expression in most contexts in this text. In some
instances it may refer to an arithmetic expression.

form

An S-expression that may be a simple constant, a variable, a simple form,
a composed form, or a special form. It may be evaluated when some correspondence has been set up between the variables contained in the S-expression
and a set of arguments. The correspondence is not part of the form.
(See function.)

free variable

A variable that is used, but not bound within the scope of an expression.
A free variable can only be determined free by considering the context in
which it appears.   In the expression

(LAMBDA (J K) (CONS J ((LAMBDA ( ) (LIST K)) ( ))))

K is a free variable in the innermost lambda expression, and a bound
variable in the outermost lambda expression.

function

An expression containing a form and a correspondence between the variables
in the form and the arguments of the function. A lambda expression is a
function, sometimes called a functional expression.

$$f = \underbrace{\lambda(x,y)}_{} \; \underbrace{y^2 + x}_{}$$

form

correspondence

$$f(1,2) = 5; \; f(2,1) = 3$$

(See also lambda notation.)

functional

A function that can have functions as arguments, e.g., MAPCAR.

functional expression

See function.

function composition

See composed forms.

global bindings

See zero-level bindings.

label notation

A scheme for temporarily naming a lambda expression, so that the expression may call itself recursively. Recursive functions call themselves by their names. Lambda expressions are functions without names. Thus, label notation gives a temporary name to a lambda expression. The notation has the form

$$(\text{LABEL name lambda-expression})$$

labels

See statement labels.

lambda conversion

The process of evaluating lambda expressions. All arguments are paired with variables in the list of variables following the LAMBDA. Then the form inside the lambda expression is evaluated using those values of the variables.

lambda expression

See lambda notation.

lambda notation

The notation first used by Church for converting forms into functions. In LISP, lambda notation is used for lambda expressions such that

$$(\text{LAMBDA } (a_1 \ a_2 \ \ldots \ a_n) \ \text{form})$$

is a function of n variables. The variables are used in the form whose arguments are the a_i. (See also function.)

lambda variable

A variable named in the list of variables following the LAMBDA in a lambda expression. (See also bound variables.)

list

A shorthand notation for an S-expression of the form

$$(s_1 . (s_2 . \ldots (s_n . NIL) \ldots))$$

This represents the list

$$(s_1 \ s_2 \ \ldots \ s_n)$$

where the s_i are any S-expressions.

list notation

A method of representing S-expressions in a convenient notation for reading and writing. (See list.)

list structure

A list of lists.

literal atom

See atomic symbol.

macro expansion

A computational process that transforms one form into some other form. The transformation rule is embedded in the definition of a LISP function. This function is invoked by the system (usually at compile-time) and given as its argument the form containing the name of the function. The value of the function is the new form which replaces the old form in whatever context the old form appeared. Generally, the transformation involves expanding the old form into a composed form of primitive function calls; however, any arbitrary computation is possible. Macros are used to define special forms in compiler-based LISP systems.

object list

A special system structure that contains all the literal atoms read by
the system. In most systems, the object list is called the OBLIST and is
manufactured by distributing the literal atoms into a series of sublists,
called buckets, by a computation (hashing) upon their Hollerith print
names. It permits fast atom recognition during reading.

ordinary variable

A synonym for bound variable.

parameters

An elementary atomic form that is either a constant or a variable.

p-list

A synonym for property list.

pointer

An internal machine address. It designates or points to a location of
interest.

predicate

In mathematics, a function, the value of which is true or false. In LISP,
a function, the value of which is T (true) or NIL (false). (See also
semi-predicate.)

print name

The original string of characters read by the system, representing the
internal name for a literal atom. This string of characters is printed
as the name of the literal atom by PRINT and other print functions.

prog expression

A synonym for program expression.

prog variable

A synonym for program variable.

program expression

An expression of the form

        (PROG (variables) statements)

that allows evaluation of statements in serial fashion. (See program
feature.)

program feature

A feature in LISP that allows programs, containing statements, to be executed in serial fashion. It also permits iteration and the use of temporary variables.

program variable

A temporary variable that is declared in the list of variables following the PROG in a program expression. Program variables are initially assigned the value NIL; however, they may be assigned arbitrary values by the pseudo-functions SET and SETQ. They are also bound and dummy variables.

property list

The list structure associated with a literal atom that may be used for storing information to be associated with the literal atom. The property list is a convenient information repository that permits rapid, dictionary-like retrieval.

pseudo-function

An expression that is called as if it were a function, but for its effect rather than for its value, e.g., READ, PRINT, DEFINE.

push-down list

The last-in-first-out (LIFO) memory area used by the system for saving partial results of recursive functions. Generalized LIFO storage for users is possible by using CONS (push) or CDR (pop) on any list.

quoting

The technique used by LISP to suppress expression evaluation. Quoting creates constant data within functions. The special form QUOTE is used for quoting.

recursion

Recursion is a technique for defining a computation on a given datum. The process usually produces a partial solution and reduces the datum to a simpler form. The same process is then reapplied to this simpler form of the datum. Again a partial solution and a simpler form are obtained. The process continues until some terminal datum obtains, whereupon all partial solutions are combined in some fashion to produce the final solution. To compute recursively the factorial of N, for example, we have

$$N! = N * (N-1)!$$

where N is the partial solution and (N-1) is the simpler form upon which we repeat the factorial computation. This process recurs until the terminal condition N = 0 is reached, whereupon the partial results are combined to form the final answer; e.g.,

$$N * (N-1) * (N-2) * \ldots 3 * 2 * 1$$

scope

The domain in which a variable is defined, i.e., its binding can be retrieved. The domain is expressed as the limits of a given expression.

semi-predicate

A function, the value of which is either NIL (false) or non-NIL (true). The implementation of COND in most LISP systems tests only for NIL. Therefore, any function that returns a value of NIL or non-NIL may be used in the predicate position of a clause of a conditional expression. CDR and SETQ are two examples of semi-predicates. (See also predicate.)

S-expression

A symbolic expression of arbitrary length that is either atomic or represents a structure having two branches at each node. The simplest form of an S-expression is an atomic symbol. A non-atomic S-expression is either:

1. A dotted pair of atoms, e.g.,

     (A . B)

   or

2. A dotted pair of S-expressions, e.g.,

     ((A . B) . C)

special cell

See value cell.

special form

A form given special treatment by LISP. It is a form having an indefinite number of arguments and/or arguments that are unevaluated and given to the special form to control evaluation.

special variable

Variables that have bindings in the value cell. They are used for constants and/or free variables. Such variables have to be declared (in some systems) before they are used with the pseudo-function SPECIAL. UNSPECIAL removes such variables from special status.

statement labels

A literal atom appearing at the top level (statement level) of a program expression is used as the name for the form following the label. This name may be used in a GO statement to transfer control to the labeled form.

statements

A series of non-atomic forms that constitute the body in a program expression. The statements are evaluated in series for their effect on variables rather than their value. All LISP forms are legal statements. Recursion is permitted. The GO and RETURN statements allow control over the sequence of statement execution.

value cell

A place used to store the value of a special variable. The value cell is associated with the literal atom name of the special variable so that the value may be retrieved by all functions, independent of context. (See zero-level bindings.)

zero-level bindings

A variable that has a value at the top level (the zero level) is bound at the top level. It has a scope that is global, i.e., may be used freely at any level since it is defined for all levels. Variables with zero level bindings are established by CSET or CSETQ (and SET and SETQ for some systems) and are usually system constants.

APPENDIX C
REFERENCES

1. John McCarthy, Paul W. Abrahams, Daniel J. Edwards, Timothy P. Hart, and Michael I. Levin, *LISP 1.5 Programmer's Manual* (Cambridge, Massachusetts: The MIT Press, 1962).

2. Timothy P. Hart and Thomas G. Evans, "Notes on Implementing LISP for the M-460 Computer." in Edmund C. Berkeley and Daniel G. Bobrow (eds.), *The Programming Language LISP: Its Operation and Applications*, 2nd ed. (Cambridge, Massachusetts: The MIT Press, 1966), p. 191.

3. Robert A. Saunders, "The LISP System for the Q-32 Computer," in Edmund C. Berkeley and Daniel G. Bobrow (eds.), *The Programming Language LISP: Its Operation and Applications*, 2nd ed. (Cambridge, Massachusetts: The MIT Press, 1966), p. 220.

4. L. Peter Deutsch and Edmund C. Berkeley, "The LISP Implementation for the PDP-1 Computer," in Edmund C. Berkeley and Daniel G. Bobrow (eds.), *The Programming Language LISP: Its Operation and Applications*, 2nd ed. (Cambridge, Massachusetts: The MIT Press, 1966), p. 326.

5. Daniel G. Bobrow, D. Lucille Darley, Daniel L. Murphy, Cynthia Solomon, and Warren Teitelman, *The BBN-LISP System* (Cambridge, Massachusetts: Bolt, Beranek and Newman, Inc., 1966), AFCRL-66-180.

6. L. P. Deutsch and B. W. Lampson, *Reference Manual, 930 LISP* (University of California, Berkeley, 1965), Document No. 30.50.40.

7. Alonzo Church, *The Calculi of Lambda-Conversion* (Princeton: Princeton University Press, 1941).

8. Richard S. Burington, *Handbook of Mathematical Tables and Formulas* (Sandusky, Ohio: Handbook Publishers, Inc., 1953), p. 45.

9. Fisher Black, "Styles of Programming in LISP," in Edmund C. Berkeley and Daniel G. Bobrow (eds.), *The Programming Language LISP: Its Operation and Applications*, 2nd ed. (Cambridge, Massachusetts: The MIT Press, 1966), p. 96.

10. Elaine Gord, "Notes on the Debugging of LISP Programs," in Edmund C. Berkeley and Daniel G. Bobrow (eds.), *The Programming Language LISP: Its Operation and Applications*, 2nd ed. (Cambridge, Massachusetts: The MIT Press, 1966), p. 93.

11. Timothy P. Hart, "MACRO Definitions for LISP" (Artificial Intelligence Project, RLE and MIT Computation Center, Memo 57, 1963).

12. J. W. Backus, "The Syntax and Semantics of the Proposed International Algebraic Language of the Zurich ACM-GAMM Conference," *Proceedings, Internat'l. Conf. Information Processing*, UNESCO, Paris, June 1959, pp. 125-132.

13. K. Samelson and F. L. Bauer, "Sequential Formula Translation," *Communications of the Association for Computing Machinery*, Vol. 3, 1960, pp. 76-83.

14. B. W. Arden, G. A. Galler and R. M. Graham, "An Algorithm for Translating Boolean Expressions," *Journal of the Association for Computing Machinery*, Vol. 9, No. 2, April 1962, pp. 222-239.

15. R. G. Toby, R. J. Bobrow and S. N. Zilles, "Automatic Simplification in FORMAC," *Proceedings, 1965 Fall Joint Computer Conference*, Vol. 27, Part 1, November 1965, pp. 37-53.

16. D. Wooldridge, "An Algebraic Simplify Program in LISP," (Artificial Intelligence Project, Stanford University, Memo 11, December 1963).

APPENDIX D
INDEX TO TECHNICAL TERMS

Function:

  name, 66

  necessary requirements, 39

Functional arguments, 137-141

Functional expression, 39-40, 53

Functionals, 137

Function definition, 39, 66

Function notation, 38

G

Garbage collector, 68, 156

Gord, Elaine, 121

I

Indicator, 150-152 (see also
      property list)

Infix notation, 163

Interpreter, 68, 115, 118, 152

L

Label notation, 98

Labels (see statement labels)

Lambda conversion, 41-43

Lambda expression:

  definition, 39-40

  evaluation, 41

  examples, 40-41

  LABEL, 98

  syntax, 40

Lambda notation, 38-45

Lambda variables, 40, 42 (see
    also variables)

LIFO, 119

List:

  circular, 145

  construction:

    APPEND, 97

    CONS, 30

    LIST, 58

    NCONC, 147

    RPLACA, 146

    RPLACD, 146

  elements, 13-14

  empty list, 14

  graphical representation, 19-22,
      144-145

  knotted, 145

  modifying structures, 146-149

  predicate functions, 77

  push-down, 119

  re-entrant, 145

  threaded, 145

  use of NIL, 14

List notation, 15-17 (see also
     S-expression)

List structure, 13, 145 (see also list)

Literal atoms, 5 (see also atomic
     symbol)

Logical connectives, 78-79

M

Macro:

  macro definitions, 152, 155

  macro expansion, 152

  nature of, 151-152

Memory management, 68

Scope:

  of expression, 43-44

  GO, 108

  RETURN, 108

  of variables, 116

Semantic errors, 122 (see also

     error)

Semi-predicate:

  application example, 164

  definition, 74

S-expression:

  building larger ones, 30-31

  definition, 6

  dot notation, 6-10

  extracting sub-expressions,

    31-33

  graphical representation, 7-10,

    19-22

  list notation, 13-22

Special cell, 117-119 (see also

    variables)

Special forms (see form)

Statement, 106-109

Statement labels, 107

String, 127-128

String quoting, 122, 128

Sub-expression (see S-expression)

Supervisors, 29-30, 130-133 (see

    also EVALQUOTE)

Symbolic expression (see S-

    expression)

Syntax errors, 121 (see also

    error)

T

Time-sharing, 121

Top-level:

  bindings, 117

  function calls, 42, 53

  list element, 77

  nature of, 132-133

  restrictions, 132-133, 141

  supervisor, 29-30, 60-63, 132-133

Trace, 124 (see also error:

    diagnostic tools)

Trees (see S-expression)

True, 74

U

Unwind, 123 (see also error:

    diagnostic tools)

V

Value cell, 117-119, 149 (see also

    variables)

Variables:

  APVAL, 117

  binding values:

    lambda conversion, 41, 117

    global bindings, 118

    on a-list, 115

    zero-level bindings, 117-118, 130

  bound variables, 114, 132

  context, 115-117

  declarations, 119

  dummy variables:

    definition, 44-45